GERMANY IN THE EARLY
MIDDLE AGES

AMS PRESS
NEW YORK

GERMANY IN THE EARLY MIDDLE AGES, 476–1250

BY WILLIAM STUBBS, D.D., FORMERLY BISHOP OF OXFORD, AND REGIUS PROFESSOR OF MODERN HISTORY IN THE UNIVERSITY OF OXFORD

EDITED BY

ARTHUR HASSALL, M.A.

STUDENT, TUTOR, AND SOMETIME CENSOR OF CHRIST CHURCH, OXFORD

WITH TWO MAPS

LONGMANS, GREEN, AND CO.

39 PATERNOSTER ROW, LONDON

NEW YORK, BOMBAY, AND CALCUTTA

1908

Library of Congress Cataloging in Publication Data

Stubbs, William, Bp. of Oxford, 1825-1901.
    Germany in the early Middle Ages,476-1250.

    Bibliography: p.
    1. Germany--History--To 1517.   I.   Title.
DD125.S75   1972   943'.02   73-38337
ISBN 0-404-06300-4

Reprinted from the edition of 1908, London

First AMS edition published in 1972

Manufactured in the United States of America

International Standard Book Number: 0-404-06300-4
Library of Congress Catalog Card Number: 73-38337

AMS PRESS INC.
NEW YORK, N.Y. 10003

PREFATORY NOTE

THE absence of satisfactory histories of Germany in the English language is as keenly felt now as it was when Bishop Stubbs was Regius Professor of Modern History at Oxford.

The present volume originated in a series of Lectures delivered in Oxford, and form a very striking sketch of the history of Germany from the days of Clovis to the thirteenth century. The reader will at once recognise that each chapter bears the impress of a master hand, and is written by one whose knowledge of the subject was profound. Being originally composed in the form of lectures, the chapters are so arranged as to prove attractive to the general reader, while the student will recognise that he has presented to him the results of laborious investigation and of a very intimate knowledge of the history of Germany. The character of each German monarch is sketched with that skill and accuracy which is so remarkable a feature of Bishop Stubbs' historical writings.

To many who associate the name of Bishop Stubbs with English History, it may be a surprise to find that he was as conversant with the history, political and constitutional, of Germany as he was with that of the British Isles.

In view of the want of a Short History of Germany in the early Middle Ages, Bishop Stubbs, some thirty-five years ago, had in contemplation the publication of a volume somewhat on the lines of the present one.

I am confident that this volume will be welcomed not only by students in the Universities and in University Colleges, but also by all who are interested in the history of Germany.

ARTHUR HASSALL.

CONTENTS

CHAPTER V

CHAPTER VI

CHAPTER VII

CHAPTER VIII

CHAPTER IX

CHAPTER X

CHAPTER XI

CHAPTER XII

MAPS

b

SOME AUTHORITIES

BRYCE : Holy Roman Empire.
BURY: History of the Later Roman Empire.
CHALANDON : Alexis Ier. Comnène.
DAVIS : Charlemagne.
EINHARD : Vita Karoli Magni.
FINLAY : History of Greece.
FISHER : The Medieval Empire.
FUSTEL DE COULANGES : Histoire des Institutions Politiques de l'Ancienne France.
GIBBON : Decline and Fall.
GIESEBRECHT : Gesch. der deutschen Kaiserzeit.
GREGOROVIUS : Gesch. der Stadt Rom im Mittelalter.
GREGORY OF TOURS : Historia Francorum.
HODGKIN : Italy and her Invaders.
—— Theodore the Goth.
LAVISSE : Histoire de France.
LAVISSE ET RAMBAUD : Histoire Générale.
LUCHAIRE : Les Communes Françaises.
MILMAN : Latin Christianity.
NITZSCH : Gesch. deutschen Volkes.
OMAN : The Dark Ages.
OTTO OF FREISING : Gesta Friderici I.
PAUL THE DEACON : Historia Langobardorum.
RANKE : Weltgeschichte.
TOUT : The Empire and the Papacy.
WAITZ : Deutsche Verfassungsgeschichte, Vol. II.
ZELLER : Histoire d'Italie.

HISTORICAL MAPS, ed. Poole (Clarendon Press).
CHRONOLOGY : Hassall, "A Handbook of European History Chronologically Arranged."

GERMANY IN THE EARLY MIDDLE AGES

INTRODUCTORY CHAPTER

NEXT to the study of the history of our own country, nearest in the degree and in the character of the interest with which it should be regarded, comes the history of Germany. I say *comes*, because in my own case I have found it so. I should perhaps say more generally, should be expected to come. For it is a melancholy fact that it does not in the ordinary process of education take this place. It might be expected that the natural advance upon the acquired knowledge of English history, the origin, the development of the institutions, and the vicissitudes of external influences which have made our nation and ourselves what we are, would be followed up by an attempt to learn the history and developments which, from the same germs, have produced so very different a nation in our German kinsmen : that we should be tempted to study the initial, fundamental basis of Teutonic institutions, which we trace in all the developments of English fortunes, in the development of German life as well ; to account for the circumstances that have made two so different trees grow apparently from the same seed if not from an identical root. There is very much *a priori* to draw us to German history in this view, and the study would involve, at least for the

A

knowledge of its outline, no very recondite research. We can see at a glance how in England every modifying influence that affected the free development of German institutions transplanted to the island soil, was still Teutonic in itself : Jute, Angle, Saxon, Dane, Norwegian, Norseman, all were Teutonic in origin, branches of one great tree of nations, springing from the stem at different heights from the ground, and therefore possessing their natural institutions, at different stages of their development, at the various periods at which they became able to affect one another directly.

In Germany itself it was otherwise. Not only was the education of the various tribes which composed the nation different from that which the conquerors of Britain had gone through, but the influences by which the nationality and the national institutions were tempered were alien to the original stock. Germany passed through a period of discipline, in her contests with Rome, which our forefathers escaped. The Angles and Saxons, from whom we spring, neither met the Roman armies in the field nor supplied the raw material for their legionaries. The impression made upon Germany, first by her struggle with Rome, then by her partial subjection and consolidation under Roman principles, then by her emancipation from Roman influences exerted directly by Romans, an emancipation won by the arms of nations, akin in origin to her own, but falling quickly into the grooves of Roman law and civilisation : an emancipation crowned by the work of the Great Charles in taking to himself the empire under which the kindred races had so long groaned, and against which the triumphant barbarians had so fiercely struggled, succumbing to the genius of the South in the midst of their victory : the reconquest of independent

Germany by the Romanised Teutons, the Franks of the empire, and the revindication by itself of the ancient nationality, although unable to eliminate the forms and laws and institutions of the Latin empire, in the long struggles of the Middle Ages;—the impression made, I say, by these changes of fortune, has been such as to render the pure German of to-day a very different being from the pure Englishman, although the one may be as purely Teutonic in blood and character and even in the fundamental principles of his constitution as the other.

From an investigation of these things much that would be of the greatest interest to Englishmen might naturally be expected. Again from the very association of the two nations in history we might gather much more : the strange phenomenon of the fertility of the transplanted genius of the race, repaying with interest its debt to the Motherland; the many ways in which England has acted upon Germany ; the fact that in the free English air, German literature first became vocal, and that the English language is the earliest literary language of the common stock, if we except the Gothic Bible of Ulfilas which belongs to a different stage, a different region, a different stock of Teutonism. From England a great part of Germany received Christianity : from England Germany received in common with the rest of the Northern Empire much of the learning and knowledge that lighted her throughout the Middle Ages: from England Germany received the inquiring and dis-puting spirit which ended in the Reformation. Wycliffe was the predecessor of Huss as Huss was the predecessor of Luther ; and Wycliffe was, so far as his education, his place as a doctor and a reformer went, a product of influences, political, literary, religious, which had been working from time immemorial in England, and which proved their kindredship to the Teutonic genius by the readiness with which they spread in Germany when the impulse was once given. The actual support given to the Reformation in Germany by England, the close alliances, formed with German states during the last three centuries, all arise almost from this and were pregnant of effects on the political state of both countries. The fact that it is from English pseudo-philosophy that the modern German pseudo-philosophy has arisen, and that in the writings of English philosophers, the religious schools of Germany have sought the antidote to the mental poison thus insinuated—all these things are full of common interest. Nor are we to shut our eyes to the other side ; to the advantages gained to England by German commerce, by German ingenuity :—the discoveries of science, the invention of the printing-press, the enormous industry and apparatus of German investigation.

All these things might seem to make German history a study almost of necessity to an Englishman wishful to acquaint himself with the influence and vicissitudes of his own country in European politics. And yet, strange as it seems, we are yet without a satisfactory History of Germany in the English language. Certain episodes of it have been written, and brilliantly written, by Englishmen. Carlyle's Life of Frederick the Great, immoral and one-sided as it most certainly is, is yet a work of great genius, of enormous industry, and of corresponding interest. But as a picture of German history it stands almost by itself ; for Robertson's Charles V.,[1] and the lucid, eloquent, touching chapters of Milman on the Church History of the land, are really of European rather than German scope, and embrace

This has now been superseded by Mr. Armstrong's Charles V.

many features, and those the most conspicuous, which are distinctly non-German, and throw the true Teutonic history into darkness and obscurity. The connection of the Empire with Germany has also had the same effect as the connection of Church History with German History. Men, in attempting to study the life of Germany, have been insensibly led off to study the history of the Empire, a subject possibly more akin to the studies for which our early classical education both in history and language have qualified us, than that of the race, however near akin and united in political and religious affinity, whose annals have to be learned through the medium of a language which must, to be acquired at all, be made the subject matter of a distinct and new industry.

Again, the study of French and Italian have until of quite late years shut out the study of German as a necessary part of the education of an accomplished man ; and, with the study of the language, the interest of the history has been excluded. So long as German was a language which did not, as it did not until the end of the eighteenth century, claim a classical character or to have a literature of its own, that was not to be wondered at ; but now Germany has a literature, if not as ancient, at least as well worth reading as that of France and Italy ; and her tongue has become, from a variety of reasons, the key to a treasury of every sort of human knowledge. Even history, even English history itself, cannot be now examined, with a due regard to the latest scholarly investigation, without recourse to German writers, such as Pauli, Gneist, Ranke, and the enthusiastic band of fellow workers. Yet, with the increased study of German as a language, we have not yet arrived at an increased and intelligent study of the history of our Teutonic kinsmen : a history which should be as interesting to us as our own is to our transatlantic cousins. For after all, the divergency created by the expanse of time that lies between English and German history, is not greater than that which is created by the distance in space and still more in ideas between us and the men of the United States. It is not indeed true of us that German history is the history of Englishmen, as English history is the history of Americans ; but it is true that the rapid extension and development of American ideas, since the Declaration of Independence, has so created a history for them, that in less than a century we shall find ourselves more closely akin, even in history and historical interests, with Germany than with America.

CHAPTER I

Germany at the Opening of the Middle Ages.—The Germany of modern history, the Germany of the Holy Roman Empire, lies partly within and partly without the general limits of the ancient or unholy Roman Empire. Taking as a rough limit the line of the Rhine and the Danube as the boundaries of the actual possessions of imperial Rome, it will be seen that all Germany east of the Rhine and north of the Danube remained practically unsubdued, or if partially subdued, unconsolidated. Great part of modern Germany lay outside the empire, and the part that lay inside it was counted to belong to provinces not in themselves radically German ; the portion of Germany west of the Rhine was accounted a part of Gaul ; and the German regions south of the Danube were for the most part regarded as Illyrian. The Germans of the heart of Germany had withstood successfully the attacks of Rome, although they had, it would seem almost of necessity, been leavened by her civilisation, and affected, after the adoption of Christianity in the empire, by the influences of her religion. Cologne, Trier, and Mainz, the three great metropolitical sees of later Germany, were Roman cities, sometimes the seats of emperors themselves ; and all had churches, founded long before the general evangelisation of Germany by Roman Christians. They were akin in habit and institutions to the churches of Gaul, and continued to be leavened by the same secular spirit throughout the Middle Ages; the Archbishops of the three great Roman cities were the spiritual electors of the heads of the Holy Roman Empire.

The Migrations.—It would be impossible, and useless if it were possible, to give in detail the migrations of the different tribes of Germany during the decline of the empire, the period that intervenes between the Germania of Tacitus and the foundation of the dominion of Clovis. They were partly the result of the state of societies emerging from barbarism : of the wandering of hunting tribes: the choosing of permanent settlement by pastoral tribes : the invasions of warlike ones : the constant draining of the more distant lands towards the empire, which by conquering and devastating regions far too wide for it to hold, was constantly leaving border lands open to the incursion of neighbour tribes, whose movements involved the movements of their neighbours behind them. So the Lombards are found moving down from the Baltic to the Danube, and the Vandals in the same way, if indeed the two sets of Vandals are really identical. After the fall of Rome before the Goths, the Huns, and the Vandals, the Eastern barbarians of kindred race experienced this result even more than the Western. Hence that Arian Christianity which had been implanted among the Goths by Ulfilas did not penetrate the nations of Western Germany to any great extent, but, being carried southwards by the Eastern barbarians, affected only the Goths, Vandals, and Burgundians : it did not affect the Franks, or the Saxons, or any of the more northern and western tribes to whom modern Germany, and indeed modern Europe, owe their history. It would be impossible to load the memory with the *minutiæ* of the internal changes of position and relation of the tribes of interior Germany between the time of Tacitus and that of Clovis; but it is necessary to have some definite idea of the relation of the nations at the latter periods, for it is a key to most of the mediæval history, and cannot be dispensed with. As we lay the foundation of the history of France by learning the position and relations of the Gallo-Romans, the Visigoths, the Burgundians, the Franks, and the Alemanni, so we lay the foundation of the history of Germany by discriminating the positions and histories of the Franks, the Saxons, the Bavarians, and the Alemanni or Swabians.

The Franks.—I. The Franks, as is learnt from Gibbon, first emerge from total darkness as a strong people in the reign of the Emperor Gallienus: from such obscurity and in such strength that it is impossible to ascribe the phenomenon to hypothetic migration, and is most reasonable to imagine that they were a confederation, or, as that word does not approve itself to modern authorities, who are strongly against the idea of federation, a combination resulting from the aggrandise-ment of a particular tribe, and known under a new name; the association, under the new name of Franks or Freemen, of the ancient Teutonic inhabitants of the lands which they then occupied in full force. This confederate or conglomerate character belonged also to the Alemanni, and in all probability to the Saxons; and must be taken for granted as an obscure but ascer-tained fact. This Frank people, into whose history it is not necessary to go further, was divided into two great branches, themselves possibly distinct agglomera-

tions with distinct history, with laws and institutions of
their own, as soon as they become *personæ* of history ;
the Salians, who occupied the present Netherlands from
the sea to the river Meuse ; and the Ripuarians, who
inhabited the country between the Meuse and the
Rhine, and the eastern bank of the Rhine as well, as
far up the stream as Cologne. Beyond them lay the
Saxons of Westphalia, while south of Cologne the
Franks extend widely towards interior Germany, with
the Main for their boundary, and the duchy of Franconia or of the East Franks remained bearing their
name down to the collapse of the empire in 1806.

The Alemanni or Swabians.—II. The confederation
or agglomeration of the Alemanni, a similar mixture
and reappearance under a collective name of the tribes
of the Suevi, had been forced south about the time of
Caracalla. By a variety of adventures, partly peaceful
and partly aggressive, they established themselves in
the south-west of Germany between the Saxon and
Frank nationalities to the north and the Burgundians
and Roman provinces to the south ; from Mainz to
the Lake of Constance to the west, as far as the river
Lech to the eastward. They thus occupied Eastern
or German Switzerland, as it is now called, and that
part of modern Germany which formerly bore the
name of Swabia, and which is now roughly represented
by the kingdom of Würtemberg and the southern part
of the Grand Duchy of Baden. Western or French
Switzerland was a part of the kingdom of the Burgundians. The name of Alemannia continued to be
given in legal documents throughout the Middle Ages
to these lands, including Alsace and Swabia, but to all
intents and purposes the name of Swabia and the
Swabians succeeds historically to its importance at an

early period, the name of Alemannia being given sometimes in Latin and almost universally in French to the
whole of Germany.

The Bavarians.—III. Beyond the Lech to the east
lay the Bavarians, Boioarians—a strong and important
nation who, like the Alemanni, had been forced into
the southern and western position as compared with
their original seats at the opening of history. The
Bavarians represent the Marcomanni, or some more
mixed agglomeration of tribes who drove the Boii, a
Gallic tribe, out of Bohemia, and becoming Boiarii
[Boi-wara] moved on into the modern Bavaria under
pressure by the Czechs. Then as now, the German
nations were bounded on the east by vast hordes of
Slavonians, and somewhat later by Tartaric or Turanian
tribes, who were gradually driving them westward, as
for the last few centuries they have themselves been
driven eastward. Under the names of Antes and
Slavonians, Slavonic tribes occupied Poland and
modern Prussia; as Wends they pressed on the
Saxons in Mecklenburg, as Czechs on the Boians in
Bohemia, and as Serbs and Slavs in Hungary on the
Illyrian provinces of Rome. The Slavonians were
themselves pressed on the east, and sometimes penetrated by the more distant Tartaric races, from which
sprang the Magyars of later Hungary. Bohemia was
the historical home of the Boii or Bavarians; forced
before the Czechs, they moved west and south into
the modern Bavaria and Austria, and there under their
king, Theodo the Agilolfing, they were established by
Theodoric, King of the Ostrogoths, as a bulwark of
his empire against the aggressions of the Franks. The
whole south of Germany, as far as the South Tyrol
southwards and Hungary eastwards, was thus Bavarian,

and continued to bear the name until the March of
Austria was created out of the eastern half of it, and the
territory assumed its modern and present dimensions.

The Saxons.—IV. The Saxons, who, like the Franks,
had probably migrated little within the historic period,
but, like the Franks and Alemanni, had substituted a
new national name for a quantity of tribal distinctions,
covered the north of Germany from the line of the
Franks and the Rhine to the neighbourhood of the
Oder eastward, where they abut in the Wends. Between
them and the Franks and Bavarians lay three or four
ancient small nations which had preserved their tribal
identity : the Chatti or Hessians, the Thuringians,
and the inhabitants of Meissen and Lausitz, Misnia
and Lusatia, which at a later period developed into
the Marches bearing those names, later still into the
electorate and duchy of Saxony, and ultimately into
the kingdom of Saxony. The country now called
Saxony was no part of the ancient territory of the
Saxons or Lower Saxony, which included Westphalia
and the territory of the kingdom of Hanover with
much that lies south of them, and thus a great part
of the kingdom of Prussia before 1866. In fact, the
kingdom of Prussia as it existed before 1866, *i.e.* the
West Prussia of Brandenburg and its accretions—not
the eastern part — roughly represented the ancient
Saxony. From the northern part of this Saxony towards Denmark, the land of the Jutes, Angles, and
Frisians, came our own forefathers in the fifth century
to Britain ; and this is the Saxonia, the old Saxony, as
it is called by Bede and the early chroniclers, which
was converted by the missions of Boniface and his
predecessors who came from the monasteries of Wessex
and Northumbria.

Summary.—These then are the materials out of which a historical nation of Germans has to be constructed: the initiation of union comes in the shape of the conqueror Clovis. Of course it will be understood that, besides these great tribal divisions, or national divisions, as they might be called, there were innumerable small tribes, some ranging under these conglomerate names, and some not included under them, but too small and obscure much to affect general history. It is upon these great ones that the Germany of history is based, and to their rivalries, their amalgamations, attractions, and repulsions that the history of Germany, read analytically, must trace the mainspring of its movements and its power, and the occasions of its weakness.

Victories of Clovis.—Clovis, whose career in its details it is unnecessary to describe, was originally King of the Salian Franks, but by his fame as a warrior and personal influence united the whole of the Franks under his sway, and began the foundation of a kingdom which developed into the Western Empire. It will be remembered how in the year 486 he vanquished Syagrius and acquired the remaining territories of Rome in Gaul: how in 496 he conquered the Alemanni at Zulpich, and in 507 the Visigoths at Vouglé. The conquest of the Burgundians was a tougher work and occupied not only himself but his successors from 499 to 532.[1]

Theodoric the Ostrogoth, 437-526.—Great, however, as Clovis was, and strangely powerful as was the impetus which survived him, he was not the arbiter of the West, nor was the Frank kingdom to approach the majesty of empire for nearly three centuries after his time. Theodoric, the great King of the Ostrogoths,

[1] See Gibbon, "History of the Decline and Fall of the Roman Empire," Cap. 38.

occupied a far more important position both before
and after the death of Clovis ; and although Theodoric
was brother-in-law to Clovis, and no doubt quite willing
that he should subdue the north, as he himself did the
south of the empire, it was by no means his purpose
that Clovis should take all. Hence, as he sustained
the Visigoths in Septimania, he sustained the Bavarians
in Germany, and it was not until after his death in
526, and the collapse of the Ostrogothic power, that
the Franks acquired even the nominal supremacy
in Gaul or in South Germany either. In Northern
Germany they were still less powerful : for the Saxons
continued in their old seats as savage and independent
as ever ; and, although the East Franks seem to have
gradually admitted the dominion of the Merovingians,
and the border states between the Saxons and the
Bavarians to have rejoiced in Frank protection, their
relations with the Bavarians themselves were anything
but heartily friendly. However, although the Burgundians continued to struggle against the Franks for
many years after the death of Clovis (in 511), the
Alemannian country seems to have been quickly consolidated, being annexed with Thuringia and Alemannia
to Austrasia, by King Theodoric, in or about 532.
The Bavarians, unsupported, gradually fell into an
uneasy sort of dependence.

The Lombards and Franks.—In the flourishing period
of the Lombards, the Franks acted occasionally as
nominal allies of the empire, which, owing to the efforts
of Belisarius, was enabled to retain a hold on Italy ;
and, so long as the Lombards were practically rivals
to the Franks, the Bavarians maintained an alliance
with the Lombards. The Lombard power, however,
declined almost as quickly as it rose (Lombard power,

sixth century), whilst that of the Franks went on increasing in spite of the weakness of the princes. By
the middle of the seventh century it may be said that
Germany, with the exception of the Saxons in the
north, was nominally Frank and nominally Christian.

Neustria and Austrasia.—But in the meantime new
names are appearing for the partitioned empire of
Clovis, and under the descendants of Clovis we find a
kingdom of Neustria and a kingdom of Austrasia added
to the ancient divisions of Aquitaine and Burgundy.
The kingdom of Neustria embraced all that part of
modern France which was not included in Aquitania
or Austrasia : it was France between the Loire and the
valley of the Meuse, the Sylva Carbonaria, north of
Ardennes, being the boundary. Austrasia comprised
the German possessions of the house, Franconia, Alemannia, the nominal command of Bavaria, and the
Ripuarian territory of Western France, including the
country which was afterwards Champagne. The division emerges about the year 561. Austrasia, of course,
was the territory of the East, or Eastern Franks, a
name which still belongs to the most Frank remnant
of it, Franconia ; the rest was Neustria, *i.e.* Non-Austria,
as it is said : Paris was the capital of Neustria, Metz
the capital of Austrasia. Of the sovereigns of either
we know little to recommend them to our memories.
What little we can retain shows that the reigning house
was subject to alternations of energy and *fainéantism,*
that it did not break up permanently into two dynasties,
but was continually being consolidated and subdivided,
and that the moral and political character of the
princes was such as combined the worst evils of barbarism with the worst evils of civilisation. It is to
Gregory of Tours that we are indebted for the most

part for our knowledge of the Merovingians ; and, as was natural, his attention is devoted far more to Neustrian than to Austrasian matters. It is thus with reference to the history of France rather than to that of Germany that he is chiefly studied. When he leaves us, we have for a long period only very scanty annals and those still French, or rather concerning what is now France.

Break-up of the Merovingian Power.—But now while the Merovingian house still retained a sort of unity, under the influence of the servants of that house, their dominion was rapidly breaking into two, nearly by the very line that in ancient times had separated the Salians from the Ripuarians, and lower down, Gaul from Germany : the empire, from the independent tribes. Though Neustria and Austrasia might often have the same king, they had two rival officers, mayors of the palace as they were called, who were gradually advancing to the position of kings and ultimately to the title of which the Merovingians were to be deprived ; and then to the empire itself. The mayor of the palace of Austrasia was the real King of Germany, the mayor of the palace of Neustria was becoming King of France. It never actually was so. Before the Merovingian house in its degradation had destroyed the unity of the Frank dominion, the mayor of the palace of Austrasia had overcome his rival and founded the house from which the Great Charles proceeded. In 638 Dagobert I., who eight years before had united the whole dominion, died, leaving Sigebert II. King of Austrasia, and Clovis II. King of Neustria and Burgundy. Sigebert had for mayor of the palace Pipin of Landen. Grimoald, Pipin's son, succeeded him as mayor ; and, on the death of Sigebert in 656, endeavoured to place his own son, Childebert, on the throne to the exclusion of Dagobert II. The attempt cost him his life. For the moment Neustria gained the supremacy with Erchinoald for sole mayor; Childeric II. and Clotaire III., the two sons of Clovis II., in the same year, 656, redivided the states, Childeric with Wulfad for mayor in Austrasia; Clotaire with Ebroin for mayor in Neustria. But the house of Pipin of Landen was not extinct; his daughter Bega married Ansegis, son of S. Arnulf, who bore the title of Duke of Austrasia, and their son, Pipin of Herstal, was nourishing deep designs. In 679, Dagobert II., the successor of Childeric, died, and Austrasia under Martin, son of Wulfad, and Pipin, son of Ansegis, refused the authority of Thierri of Neustria, wielded by the mayor Ebroin. In a battle in 680 near Laon, Ebroin beat his rivals, but did not live long enough to recover Austrasia; he died in 681. For six years Pipin, who had rid himself of his colleague Martin, governed alone; in 687 he beat Berthaire, the mayor of the palace of Neustria, at the battle of Testri, and took the king prisoner. Henceforth, although mayors for Neustria are still appointed, they are appointed by Pipin. In 714 he appointed his grandson, a boy of six years old, mayor to the king, Dagobert III., who was fifteen : one phantom, as Montesquieu says, set over another phantom : he himself governed Austrasia for thirty-four years, and the whole Frank dominion for twenty-seven. He died in December 714. The same year was born the third and greatest Pipin, son of Charles Martel, and father of Charles the Great.

Germany, Bavaria.—In these dreary details we see little of Germany. The internal struggles of the Frank monarchy occupy the whole energy of the mayors. But for this, the lingering remnant of Lombard empire,

B

and the Exarchate of Ravenna itself, must have long ago fallen before the energy of the North German races. But now the Agilolfings in Bavaria were drawing nearer to the Lombards, and even aspiring to act as arbiters between the two races. In 708 Theodo IV. was strong enough to place his own ward Liutpert on the throne of Lombardy, and drew the cords of alliance closer. But the power of the Austrasian princes for half a century before this had been defied by the Bavarians. King Dagobert, between 630 and 638, had reformed the Bavarian laws ; but this was the last act of authority exercised by the Merovingians.[1] Theodo VI., who reigned from 653 to 660, although bearing only the title of Duke, governed his states without any pretence of subordination to the King or Government at Metz ; and his descendants persevered in the same independent course, until they were conquered by Charles Martel. To this point then there is very little on which much criticism can be bestowed. Saxony is still heathen and independent. Alemannia is consolidated with Franconia as the territory of the kings of Austrasia at Metz. Bavaria has obtained a prescriptive but precarious independence. In the next chapter an attempt will be made to clear the way towards the appreciation of the position of Germany under the Great Charles.

[1] Theodo III., who became Duke of Bavaria in 612, married a daughter of King Theodebert of Austrasia and became a Christian.

IMPORTANT DATES

Clovis, 481–511.
Theodoric the Ostrogoth, 487–526.
Dagobert, 628–638.
The Rois Fainéants, 639–752.

CHAPTER II

The Situation under the later Merovings.—There are
one or two considerations which ought not to be over-
looked. In the first place, although it is a great
mistake to regard the Merovings and the house of Pipin
from which Charles sprang as French in the modern
sense of the word, or indeed as anything but German
in every sense, it is nevertheless certain that Neustria
or modern France was much more completely subject
to them, and more thoroughly and regularly organised
than Austrasia, much more than those further portions
of the German land which, like Bavaria, lay practically
beyond the limits of the Austrasian half of the dominion.
Saxony and Thuringia were frequently at open war
with the Franks ; while Bavaria, only in very imperfect
subjection and that under a brave race of native princes,
was strong in foreign alliances and deemed herself, as
a nationality and a national sovereignty, nowise inferior
to the descendants of Clovis. German or Eastern
France had indeed been without that civilisation and
training that Neustria had had from the Romans, and,
with the exception of the close neighbourhood of the
Rhine, was far more thinly inhabited and far more

purely German than any portion of the western kingdom. The difficulties of the Merovingians in Germany
were then owing rather to imperfect civilisation and
neighbour war than to the internal and more political
quarrels, which were the result of a higher organised
and more ancient civilisation in the other half. The
dynastic quarrels and the political or open struggles
for the mayoralty and for the substance of royal power
took place accordingly either in Neustria or in that part
of Austrasia which was most like Neustria—the western
and more anciently settled territory on the Rhine.
Hence in Germany proper we have much less incident,
and much less interesting incident.

The Fall of the Merovings.—Another point closely connected with this is that, although we regard the Merovingians as permanently and finally set aside by Charles
Martel (although not formally disposed of until the
following reign), we are not to suppose that this arrangement was acquiesced in at all pleasantly or succeeded
by a season of perfect peace. It was far otherwise :
the reign of Charles Martel was a continual series of
struggles. The great territory of Aquitaine was still
possessed by a branch of the Merovingians which did
not share the general decadence of the family, and
this was a source of difficulty down even into the
reign of Charles the Great. But even the *roi fainéant*
of Noyon and Metz was not entirely a puppet, or at
least a puppet of Charles Martel, and had still rival
mayors of the palace to set up in opposition to the
Duke of Austrasia. The result of this is that although
Charles and his house were decidedly Austrasian or
German in original position, the greatest part of their
action lies in Neustria ; and Germany proper has less
recorded history now than it deserves. Several isolated

campaigns were fought by Charles with the Frisians, the Saxons, and the Bavarians, which may be summed up briefly; but on the whole it is not surprising that Frenchmen and indeed some historians regard both him and Pipin as Frenchmen. Their bones lie in the great sanctuary of the French at S. Denys, and the great exploit by which Charles is best remembered, the battle of Tours against the Moors, and his great constitutional act, the secularisations of church property, belong to Western France. Charles the Great, on the other hand, was a German of the Germans in life and death.

The Reign of Charles Martel, 715–741.—The reign of Charles Martel lasted from 715–741 :[1] during that time, besides his more famous wars with Aquitaine and with the Moorish invaders, and his constant, internal difficulties, he fought the following campaigns with the independent Germans. In 716 he was attacked by the Frisians under Radbod their king, and the same year by the Saxons. He seems to have been actually beaten by the Frisians. He was then in fact in his greatest difficulties, the Merovingian king being still powerful on the Rhine. Having, however, in 716, got possession of Cologne and of the treasures of his father Pipin, he administered a severe rebuke to the Saxons, overrunning their country as far as the Weser. In 725 he brought the Bavarians under his sway : defeated the Dukes Grimoald and Hugobert, and humbled them so thoroughly that they did not venture to stir during the remainder of his reign. He himself, to secure the peace, married a Bavarian princess, and

---

[1]
CHARLES MARTEL, *d.* 741

| Carloman | Pipin le Bref, King 752-768 |

Charles the Great, 768-814

gave one of his daughters as wife to Odilo, the son of
Hugobert, who succeeded to the Bavarian throne in
739. In 732, at the battle of Poitiers, he overthrew
the Arabs and saved Aquitaine. In 733 he defeated
and slew Poppo, Duke or King of the Frisians; in 734
he again defeated them. In 738 he conquered and
made tributary the whole of the south of Westphalia,
between the Lippe and the Rhine. In 741 he died,
leaving his dominions between his sons Pipin and
Carloman—Pipin to have Neustria, Burgundy, and
Provence; Carloman to have Austrasia, Alemannia, and
Thuringia, with of course the later conquests of his
father from the Saxons and Frisians.

The Conversion of Germany.—But although in one
sense these events are nearly all that is known of
Germany during this period, in another sense it becomes apparent that a very important change was
going on amongst the independent nations. They
were being Christianised. The reign of Charles Martel
and Pipin is in fact the great and most brilliant period
of the missionary exertion of the Anglo-Saxon Church,
and it was to Friesland and Saxony that her missions
were sent. The missions of the Northumbrian Church
were directed to Holland as it now is, North and
Western Frisia, and resulted in the formation of the
Church of Utrecht, the Mother Church of the Netherlands; the missions of the Scots were directed to the
more southern parts of Germany, Franconia, Bavaria,
and the mountains of Alemannia, and may be regarded
as represented by the Churches of Würzburg, Salzburg,
and Saint Gallen. The West Saxon missions went
to the old Saxon and the East Frisians, under Boniface,
the great English martyr of the eighth century, who
was not only a great missionary, but a great reformer

of the French and German Churches ; who baptized
Charles the Great, consecrated Pipin to the kingdom,
and who, as much perhaps as any man, contributed to
bring about that accord between the Court of Rome
and the family of Pipin which ultimately resulted in
the establishment of the empire in the person of his
son. There can be no doubt that the conversion of
interior and northern Germany was a far greater step
towards the consolidation of the empire than any
cursory exploits of Charles Martel, but the effect was
not yet apparent, and even thirty years after the death
of Charles very much remained to be done.

The Reign of Pipin and Carloman, 741–747.—Pipin
and Carloman reigned jointly from 741 to 747, when
the sovereign of Austrasia retired to Monte Casino
(on the plan of the English, and especially the Northumbrian and West Saxon princes, who had exchanged
the crown for the tonsure). During these six years
he signalised himself as a warrior little less than did
his brother ; joined Pipin in plundering their third
brother Grippo of the small territory bequeathed by
his father, and in humbling in Neustria and Austrasia,
in Aquitaine and Germany, the enemies of the house.
In particular, Dietrich, King of the Saxons, who maintained a brave and obstinate resistance, was defeated
by Carloman in 743, and taken prisoner in 744.   In
745 Saxony was again attacked, and the people to
some extent compelled to receive baptism. Odilo,
Duke of Bavaria, was also attacked, notwithstanding a
strong papal inhibition in 743, and only allowed to
retain his dominions at the intercession of his wife,
the sister of Pipin and Carloman.[1]

Pipin le Bref, sole King, 751–768.—In 751 Childeric

---

[1] In 747 Carloman, after a vigorous reign, abdicated.

was deposed, and that year saw Pipin sole sovereign
of the domains of his house. For several years he continued an aggressive policy. Grippo, his brother, whom
he had released after the resignation of Carloman, fled
from him to Bavaria, the administration of which he
usurped after the death of Odilo. The struggle in
Bavaria lasted until 751, when Pipin overcame Grippo
and restored his nephew Thassilo. Before going into
Bavaria, Grippo had raised the Saxons against Pipin,
subjected the valiant Dietrich to a third imprisonment, and having exhausted and ruined his friends in
Germany he retired to Aquitaine and fomented war
there. Ultimately he perished in Lombardy in 753.
But now Pipin was setting his mind on still greater
things, and, in the assumption of the title of king,
and in protection of the interests of the Pope, was
opening up a new region of conquest and danger,
which for a time again obscured the interests of
Germany. In 752 he was consecrated King of the
Franks by S. Boniface at Soissons; in 754 he was
reconsecrated by Pope Stephen II. at S. Denis; in
755 he invaded Lombardy and compelled Aistulfus to
promise the cession of his conquests. In 756 he put
an end to the exarchate of Ravenna, the dominion of
the empire of Constantinople in Italy, and by giving
it to the Pope laid the foundation of the temporal
power of the Papacy. The remaining years of Pipin
were taken up by wars in Saxony and Aquitaine, which
he did not succeed in entirely subjugating. The war
with Saxony, however, was continued in a chronic
struggle from year to year; in 755 Boniface suffered
martyrdom in Friesland; in 757 Pipin received the
solemn homage of Thassilo and all the Bavarian chieftains in a great assembly at Compiègne; in 758, after

obtaining a victory, he compelled the Saxons to pay a tribute of three hundred horses annually; from 760 to 763 he was engaged in war with Aquitaine. In 763 Thassilo deserted him and never returned to his allegiance. Pipin indeed made preparations for reducing him to order, but year after year passed before he could carry out his intention. Pipin died on the 24th of September 768, leaving a thick crop of troubles for Charles and Carloman.

Charles the Great and Carloman, 768.—It can hardly be said that Pipin's reign had much altered the position of the eastern kingdom. Vast as was the increase of the power of his house, by the adhesion of the Papacy and by the humiliation of the Lombards, the line of the frontier in Germany was very little advanced beyond what Clovis had left it, and the attitude of the German provinces was not less threatening. The young princes, on their accession, saw the work of a lifetime before them; Aquitaine still Merovingian and hostile; Saxony still heathen and equally hostile; Bavaria arming and fortifying for independence; Lombardy waiting for revenge; and, to crown all, a more complete confederacy of these foes than had ever before existed. Charles was the eldest son, but as usual the domains were divided. To Carloman fell Austrasia and North Neustria, and to Charles Southern Neustria and Burgundy. Aquitaine, as yet unconsolidated, was to be a common burden. Carloman was accepted as king at Soissons, Charles at Noyon. In 771 Charles married, in opposition to the Pope's advice, the daughter of the Lombard king Desiderius. In December of the same year Carloman died, and his brother, disregarding the very problematical rights of his children, succeeded to the whole empire of the Franks.

Charles, sole King, 771-814.—It is impossible to over-rate the importance of the position and character of Charles in its relation to the whole history of the Middle Ages. There is, in Eginhard, a very succinct and clear account of his several wars. Although several of these wars have no immediate concern with Germany, nearly all are in some way connected by the network of Lombard policy, and, until the Lombard kingdom was finally extinguished, the domestic policy of Charles can be only very scantily discovered and still more scantily indicated. Charles, as has been stated, had married a daughter of Desiderius ; a year after his marriage he returned her to her father. Whatever may have been his reason for returning her, policy might have made him keep her ; for not only by the alliance did he secure the friendship of his most powerful rival, and, by that means, opportunity for the entire consolidation of his dominions, but he held in his hand the thread of a family confederacy. Luitburga, one of her sisters, was the wife of Thassilo, the revolted Duke of Bavaria ; another was married to Aragis, Duke of Beneventum, a very dangerous neighbour to Charles's friend the Pope. Aquitaine was also on the closest terms of friendship with Lombardy. To Lombardy, accordingly, the widow and children of Carloman fled for protection after his death, and the repudiation of Desiderata or Hermengard. This Lombard connexion gives a clue to the early wars of Charles.

The Wars of Charles in Aquitaine, Italy, and Saxony.—The first war was the Aquitanian, which took place in 769 before the death of Carloman. It nowhere touches German history. The Lombard war succeeds, and lasts until Desiderius is beaten in 774 and his son Adalgis taken as a hostage. The Lombard empire, after two hundred and six years of existence, ends with Desiderius' defeat in 774; the Lombard state of Friuli survived until 776, Spoleto to 773. Whilst the Lombard war was raging, the Saxon war began in 772 and lasted off and on for thirty-three years. Setting it aside for the moment, we pass over the Spanish war in 778, the Breton war and the Italian war against the remnant of the Lombard power in South Italy, which took Charles the third time to Rome in 787. In all these Charles obtained a victory which, whether easy or not, was apparently final, and which placed France and Italy very completely at his feet. It was altogether different in Germany. The Saxon is not the only war on the Austrasian frontier: we have also the Bavarian, the Slavic, the Avar and Hunnic, the Bohemian and Livonian wars. Forty-seven years in all they lasted, and at the end he had increased his dominions by the acquisition of Saxony, which, Eginhard tells us, is twice as large as Franconia and of Pannonia, Danubian Dacia, Histria, Liburnia and Dalmatia. Besides these, in Germany itself he had subdued the barbarous nations between the Rhine and the Vistula, the Welatabi, Sorabi, Abotrites, and Boemanni. In France he had secured Aquitaine, Italy as far as Calabria, and Spain as far as the Ebro.[1]

The Character of Charles' Conquests.—It is now necessary to ascertain by what means he gained so large a territory in Germany, and what was the real character of his tenure of it, for it is impossible to regard it as equable throughout, or in the more distant borders as anything more than either a nominal submission, or the

---

[1] In 778 Charles invaded Spain and extended his boundary to the Ebro. The famous Roland died in an engagement in the Pass of Roncesvalles during Charles's retreat.

enforcement of occasional obedience by ravaging expedition. There is, however, no doubt but that on every side Charles pushed the dominion of the German nation further than it had ever yet extended. He did not content himself with merely subduing the kindred races, such as the Bavarians and Saxons, but humbled their still more warlike and alien neighbours: the Slavs beyond Saxony; the Scandinavians beyond Frisia; the Avars and Huns beyond Bavaria; the still more barbarous and possibly Tartar hordes to the south of Hungary and the neighbourhood of the Hadriatic.

The Saxon Wars, 772–804.—The Saxon war began, or rather the Saxon Conquest, for war was the normal relation, was undertaken definitely in 772. Charles got together a great assembly at Worms, entered the Saxon territory, took Eresburg and overthrew the Irminsul, then proceeded as far as the Weser, where he received the submission of the people. This campaign permanently added a portion of Westphalia to the kingdom. But whilst the Lombard war was straining every nerve of Charles's power, in 774 the Saxons again began hostilities by invading Hesse, and retaliating for the overthrow of the Irminsul, by the demolition of the Church of S. Boniface at Fritzlar, which was only prevented by a panic, caused, according to the annalist, by divine interposition. As soon as the Lombard war was over Charles sent three armies into Saxony, and devastated the country, carrying off great booty. The following year, 775, he subdued Engria and Westphalia, the remaining parts of Saxony, advanced as far as Lübeck northwards, and, after a very narrow escape from the active and now experienced foe, retired into his own dominions having taken hostages of the Westphalians. In 776 the war was again in Westphalia.

Charles was recalled from Italy by the attack of the
Saxons, who destroyed the fortifications he had built to
overawe them.   In 777, at a great Diet at Paderborn, he
received the submission of all the chieftains except
Witikind : it was there that he received the invitation to
the Spanish war, which occupied him in 778.   Of his
absence in Spain the Saxons took advantage so far as to
push on to the Rhine.   But it is hardly any use to
repeat the same thing year after year.   Every season
Westphalia is invaded by the Saxons and reconquered
by the Franks.   In 780 Charles advanced to the Elbe :
in 782 he held a national council in the heart of Westphalia.   Each time, as soon as his back was turned, the
indefatigable Witikind returned to the charge and undid
what the king had done.   In this latter year, 782, a
great expedition, projected against the Slav population
beyond the Elbe, was arrested and defeated by the
Saxons on the Weser, with great slaughter, which was
avenged by a cruel massacre of four thousand and five
hundred Saxons by Charles's command at Verden on the
Aller.   The year 783[1] began with a continuance of the
war.   Having defeated the Saxons at Detmold, Charles
proceeded to Paderborn, and there heard that they were
waiting to give him battle on the Hase near Osnabrück.
There he won a second great battle, and these were the
only two, Eginhard remarks, in which he personally
took part during the whole Saxon war.   The principal
part of the war of 784 was managed by his son Karl,
but late in the year the king himself advanced into the
heart of Saxony and spent the winter at Eresburg, holding his great spring assembly again at Paderborn.

The Pacification of Saxony, 785–804.—This apparent
permanent occupation of their territories seems to have

---

[1] In that year his wife Hildegarde died and Charles married Fastrade.

exhausted the spirit of the Saxons; and they prepared
to submit. Witikind and Abbio, their leaders, were
persuaded to reconcile themselves with the king, and
they were brought to him at Attigni and there baptized.
From that date Saxony formed a part of the Frank
empire, and, although there were occasional renewals
of war down to 804, they were not such as to call for
more than passing notice. Charles, as soon as the submission of the natives was complete, set himself to
reorganise the administration and to strengthen the
Church; divided the country into eight bishoprics,
and appointed a Count Trutman to preside in the provincial assemblies, protect the clergy, and direct the
administration of justice. To Witikind, it is said that
he left the duchy of Engria, the middle portion of
Westphalia; and this would have been in agreement
with the usual policy of the German conquerors, but
it is not quite certain : the laws, however, which were
drawn up for Saxony are extant, and partake largely
of the character of the jurisprudence that would be
required by a nation at once conquered, Christianised,
and civilised. This organisation seems to have been
completed by the year 789. The new laws do not, however, quite lead us to suppose that the people for whom
they were enacted were mere barbarians, for they contain an enactment on the point of perjury, which
simply confirms the old custom of the nation; and
of course other points of that custom, untouched by
these laws, would remain in full force. The last of
the laws forbids the holding of assemblies without
the presence of the king's representative.

Annexation of Bavaria, 788.—But before the pacification of Saxony was thus completed, war or rebellion,
if we choose to call it so, had broken out in the south.

As early as 785 there had been a great conspiracy against Charles in Franconia under Count Hardrad, which was suppressed only by great promptness and cruelty ; but the real danger arose from the still hostile position of Bavaria, where Thassilo still held out in sulky independence, forgetful of the oath that he had taken to Charles when a boy, and prompted by his wife to avenge if possible the injuries of the Lombards. In the year 781, whilst he was at Rome, Charles had agreed with the Pope Hadrian to send an embassy to Thassilo, which resulted in his attending at Worms and renewing his oath, but he very soon relapsed into his former attitude. For nearly three hundred years, this had been the attitude of Bavaria, which was an enormous state, occupying the whole of modern Bavaria and the German states of Austria as far as the frontiers of Hungary. It was now being Christianised and rapidly civilised, but it had not strength or consistency to withstand the hostility of the Franks, and had been maintained in its semi-independence first by the balance of power created by the Ostrogoths, who may be said to have established it, and after their fall by a similar relation with the Lombards. It was not like Franconia or Alemannia, which were provinces of the Frank dominion : for Bavaria had never been reduced absolutely to this state; its kings or dukes were rather subject allies of the Frank sovereigns than actual officers, even after they had begun to be regarded as a part of the empire. The Frank king named, or rather recognised, the Bavarian duke at each vacancy, and had a right of supreme justice where he could enforce it ; otherwise the administration was carried on independently on the ancient national system. The position was thus intermediate between the entire ex-

emption enjoyed by the Saxons and the entire subjection of the East Franks and Swabians. This position
Bavaria was now to lose, and by that loss to give some
sort of unity and symmetry to the German possessions
of the house of Pipin. Thassilo had lost his last external safeguard in the destruction of the Lombard
kingdom, and was not wise enough to continue faithful
to the new lord of the West, to whom he was bound
both by cousinship and by the most solemn oaths
more than once repeated. He now formed a league
with the Huns and Avars, his neighbours in Pannonia,
with the Lombards of Beneventum, and with the
Empress Irene. These manœuvres reached the ears
of Charles, and as soon as he returned from Italy in
787 he began to look towards Bavaria. Thassilo in
vain attempted to get a reconciliation by the aid of
the Pope. His ambassadors were found to be without
proper powers, and this by itself was an argument of
bad faith. Charles advanced to Augsburg, which was
close on the Bavarian frontier, and there met Thassilo,
who for the third time took oaths and gave hostages.
The next spring, 788, Charles called a general assembly
of the whole of his empire at Ingelheim, which was
attended by representatives of all the nations under
his sway, the Saxons, Alemanni, Bavarians, and Lombards. There Thassilo was accused, by the Bavarians
themselves, of treason against Charles : he was condemned to death ; but Charles spared his life and sent
him into a monastery, annexing his states as a permanent province to the kingdom.

War with the Huns and the Avars, 788–797.—The
Huns and Avars, faithful to their agreement with Thassilo, now undertook to avenge him, or rather perhaps to
prevent their own impending subjugation, and invaded

both Bavaria and the duchy (march) of Friuli, which Charles had acquired from the Lombards. The war with these barbarians lasted eight years; it was chiefly carried on by Pipin the son of Charles, and the result of it seems to have been to reduce the Hungarians to something like the position which the Bavarians had hitherto occupied. And the same may be said of the war with the Slavs on the other side of the Elbe; they were humiliated, half conquered, and half Christianised, but not so thoroughly amalgamated or organised as were the Saxon and Bavarian population, nor were they ever so regularly and formally a portion of the Frank empire as the interior states became.[1] Bohemia was rendered tributary also by Charles, but it was not Christianised for a long time to come, and cannot be regarded as more than nominally conquered. These border states, at the utmost estimate of their subject character, were different from Bavaria in its former condition, in this that they were still heathen, and so had neither the advantages nor the disadvantages of a common religion with their conquerors.

Position of Charles in Germany in 790.—Thus, by the year 790, Charles the Great saw himself at the head of the whole of the German tribes; of all the Teutonic tribes except the Scandinavians, for his dominion did not extend northwards into Denmark. Lübeck is probably as far north as he reached towards Denmark; the great Lüneburg heath was the actual, although the river Eyder may have been nominally the limit of the empire. Eginhard gives an account of a Danish war, in which Godfred, the King of the Danes, attempted to push

---

[1] In discussing the history of the Ottos the subject of the Hungarians will be returned to, and when we come down to the times of Frederick Barbarossa and Henry the Lion that of the Slavs will be discussed.

through Friesland and Lower Saxony to Aix-la-Chapelle, but was prevented by death (810). His successor, Heming, accepted the Eyder boundary. It should be added, that whilst the war with the Slavs and Wends was carried on only by Charles the son of the king, that in Hungary was carried on only by Pipin, whilst Lewis acted as his father's lieutenant in France and on the Spanish march. Lewis was at his birth created King of Aquitaine; Pipin from the year 781 was called King of Italy; and Charles, King of Franconia. Already the plan of empire was being marked out for the father. The year 790 is a convenient date for the subjection of Germany, because by that time all was formally incorporated under Charles; but several severe campaigns were fought with Saxons before the year 804, when the Saxon war is counted by Eginhard to have terminated. Still, from the deposition of Thassilo, and the organisation of Saxony and Bavaria under new laws, the future kingdom of Germany was completed. At this point, it is convenient to take a review of the state of affairs before the coronation of Charles as emperor, as successor to the status of Augustus and Constantine, and the consequent involution of Germany with the general politics of Europe in a way in which no other state was ever so involved; the imperialising of Germany and Germanising of the empire, which must be the matter for discussion in future lectures.

The Character and Position of Charles the First.—What was the real character of this German kingdom before the assumption of the empire, and, with the imperial title, some shadow of imperial forms and principles of government? Charles has been called a German of the Germans, in opposition to his forefathers, who were rather Franks than Germans in the broad sense.

It may seem fanciful to do this ; but whatever the
truth of the thing may be in itself, so far as the
opinion and fame of after ages goes, such he was.
His grand, stern, rugged figure stands out Titanic
throughout the Middle Ages : there is no one like him
after him, few enough like him before, and none so
great as he. Not free from the pride, lust, and cruelty
of conquerors, he is yet singularly free from the errors,
misfortunes, and crimes into which such passions lead
conquerors. A persecutor he was, perhaps, when a
king who was a missionary and a civiliser could hardly
fail to persecute ; an oppressor, perhaps, where oppres-
sion is the only guarantee of order. In many respects
he might have been a better man ; and if a better then
also a greater : but he was both better and greater than
those who came before or after. We cannot wonder
that he is the hero of two mighty nations, the hero of
their mythical as well as of their true history ; the
central figure of their Pantheon and Walhalla.

Charles a German.—To what extent was Charles a
German hero ? Certainly not in the sense in which
either Egbert or Alfred was an English one. His birth
as Frank was pure German ; his favourite home of
Aachen or Aix-la-Chapelle was a purely German home.
But he was not the chosen representative of the German
race. He was a German conqueror of Germans, *i.e.* a
Frank conqueror of Bavarians and Saxons. He did
not reunite the divided elements of a single nationality ;
Germany had never been one before him, as it really
has never been one after him. Never in historic times
had the Bavarians and the Saxons been one nation ; the
case of England, with its several kingdoms united by
Egbert and Athelstan, is very different. Their people
were of one race ; their kings descendants of one

Woden ; their religion had come to them from the same
commingled stream, and had made them one Church
before they became one State. But Germany had no
such bond of union, nor was the empire of Charles the
expression of any yearning for such union ; it was not
even acquiesced in as satisfying such a want as it
seemed to create. The Saxons and Bavarians were
opposed as heathens to Christians ; the Bavarians and
Franconians received their Christianity from a different
source : the West and East Franks were rival races
from the beginning of history. Setting aside the
Neustrian and Burgundian states, and in regarding
Charles as a German, we must not fall into the corresponding error to that of those who regard him as exclusively a Frenchman.

The Population of Neustria mainly Celtic.—As a Frank
he was at the head of two great kingdoms, to which the
name of Neustria and Austrasia may be broadly given,
or France and Germany. Of these, Neustria or France
possessed the older organisation : it had shared the
civilisation of Rome ; it had enjoyed such settled
government as was possible under the Merovingian
rule ; it was more compact, above all, there was as yet
no rival power to that of the sovereign. The bishoprics
and the secular magistracies were arranged and divided
on the lines of imperial Rome, or on the still more
ancient lines that imperial Rome had been herself
guided by. But the population was not Frank; the
basis of it was still as Celtic as it had been in the time of
Cæsar. The towns were indeed full of Roman families ;
the Latin language was the language of the courts and
literature ; even the Visigoths used the law of imperial
Rome in the Code of Theodosius, and unquestionably
great parts of the Frank law was derived from the same

source; the bishops chosen from the leading burgher (*i.e.* Roman) families, use Roman names and cultivate Roman literature. Rome had, after the invasion of the barbarians, a stronger hold on France than on Italy; and the Franks were themselves attached to Roman traditions much more than any of the other German races. Franks had fought with Rome against Attila; Franks had resisted the Goths and Lombards; Clovis himself had been proud to take a Roman title, and Brunechild had had a persistent Roman policy of despotism and centralisation. But supposing that political principles and associations like these had a corresponding weight in Austrasia to what they had in Neustria, still Austrasia was but a small part of the Germany of Charles.

The Population of Austrasia were German.—But the population of Austrasia, at least of Franconia and Alemannia, was far more thoroughly German than that of Neustria, and of course the countries that he conquered were pure. I take it to be rather true that Charles made Germany than that Germany produced Charles; and that his greatness as a German consists largely in his forgetting that he was a Frank, and in at once admitting all his German conquests to a condition of freedom, right, and equality, which obtained for him the credit of a founder and a lawgiver. It was not that he united a divided family, but that he made into a family a group of nations that had for centuries been hostile and jealous, that had in their divergency of dialect, religion, and institutions altogether lost sight of that original primeval unity of blood, which he recognised, and on which he hoped to work for a true and corporate unity. This combination, unity of race with persistent opposition in laws, language, institutions, religion, and political affinities, is the great problem of German history which even Charles failed to solve.

IMPORTANT DATES

Charles Martel, 715–741.
War with the Bavarians, 725.
Battle of Poitiers, 732.
Pipin the Short, 752–768.
Charles the Great, 768–814.
Death of Carloman, 771.
Beginning of the Saxon Wars, 772.
Charles King of Italy, 774.
Charles invades Spain ; battle of Roncesvalles, 778.
Deposition of the Duke of Bavaria, 788.

CHAPTER III

Charles the Great as Emperor.—From the year 768
to 800, Charles the son of Pipin governed the states
which he inherited as king of the Franks, and those
which he had conquered as king of the nations that
composed them ; he was king of the Lombards from
785, as he had been king of the Franks before ; and
the acquisitions he made in Germany were regarded
as extensions or revindications of the rights of the
Frank supremacy. From the year 800 to his death,
he governed as emperor most serene of the Romans
as Cæsar and Augustus ; "as crowned by God," the
great pacific emperor governing the Roman empire,
who also by the mercy of God was king of the Franks
and Lombards. Into this eminence he had entered
by default of the Cæsars of Byzantium, as his father
Pipin had entered on the kingdom of Clovis by default
of the Merovingians ; in both cases the symbol of
dominion had come from the Pope, and in both for
some eminent service done by the Frank to the Pope
in great peril. To a man at once so politic, so honest,
and so strong as Charles was, the title of emperor
could bring little access of power : it brought no
accession of dominion ; it involved no change in the

relation between himself and the nations he governed before; it was but the crowning of the supreme power by the supreme title, and the recognition by the Eternal City of the authority of a prince, but for whose help the eternity would have become a nonentity. It might impose on the barbarous nations whom he had checked, and to whom the name of Cæsar had traditional terrors, but it could do, in his person, little else; all the substance of power he had before. Charles does not sink his titles either as hereditary king or conqueror in the more imposing one, but, as in his own description of himself, which I have read, preserves the mention of Franks and Lombards although giving precedence to the imperial name. There is not too much in a name; but, if we would rightly understand the form, we must remember that all the German nations, united under the name of Franks, entered into the rights of Franks. The Saxons and Bavarians are counted to have become Franks by the conquest, but neither they nor the original Franks are to be regarded as sunk in the empire, under Charles at least.

Charles' Title of Emperor : the year 800.—The word emperor might be an unique title of the right of universal empire, but Charles knew that he was emperor because he was king of the Franks and Lombards; he knew that the Franks and Lombards owed him no more binding allegiance as emperor than as king. He continued to govern as a king; he issued his capitularies as the kings before him had done; he governed by dukes and counts; he held his great *placita* twice in the year; he made no innovations from the imperial law; he did but strike his money in his imperial name. Hallam recognises this in the sentence in which he declares that Charles continued to be a

German and not a Roman sovereign, and adds that throughout the period of the Karolings the same German character continued. Yet from this date, 800, begins the long period during which the imperial name and its accompanying rights, varying constantly with the power of the bearer, become inseparable ; in which we see the title given only to German sovereigns, and the only dominions which practically it conveys German dominions ; a fact which almost seems to justify the vulgar error of regarding the empire as German rather than Roman, and speaking of the Holy Roman Emperor as Emperor of Germany. The lesson of the ninth century regarding Germany is the tracing of the process by which this great country, far the largest part of which had never belonged to the old empire, now became imperial, and so much so that it was able to retain for its sovereigns the title of emperor so long as it continued to be worth holding.

The Question of the Succession.—Charles survived all his sons except one, Lewis the Pious, who succeeded him in the empire. Whilst his elder sons, Charles and Pipin, were alive, they had borne titular royalty as Lewis himself did. The three were kings of Franconia, Italy, and Aquitaine ; new titles, having no reference to the ancient rights which the father had conquered, but invented by him to give additional honour to the really ducal jurisdiction which they occupied under him. As a Frank he could not but look forward to the partition which, according to all precedent, would be made of his dominions after his death. As the sons of Clovis and of Clotaire had divided their inherit-ance ; as Pipin and Carloman, his father and uncle, had divided theirs ; as he himself and his brother Carloman had done in their turn, so Charles, Pipin, and Lewis

would, when he should die. He might see that it
would be far better otherwise, that the nations whom
he was trying to make one should continue to be
one; and that the principle of Unity, which he might
esteem himself to have obtained with the title of emperor, should live on. The prestige of the imperial
title might supply a basis of cohesion; the kings of
the Franks need no longer be opposed to one another,
equally independent and jealous, at Soissons and Noyon,
at Paris and at Aix-la-Chapelle; but one might be
emperor and keep a hand, if not of actual authority,
at least of moral arbitration and restraint; nay, why
should not one be emperor and suzerain and the others
his allied and titularly subject princes? If such a
plan had been devised and could have been carried
out, it would have been a perfect development of the
feudal principle applied to the highest subject matter.
It may have been the idea of Charles, as it was of
Lewis within a few years of his father's death; but the
necessity for such a device did not press on Charles:
his son Pipin died in 810; Charles died in 811; Lewis
only survived; and on Lewis, subject only to the provision made for Bernard, son of Pipin, as King of Italy,
devolved the accumulated honours of his father. We
have not, however, to depend on conjecture for the
details of the scheme which commended itself to Charles'
mind, whilst his sons were alive.

Charles' Proposed Division of his Empire. — In the
year 806 Charles published a capitulary in which he
divides his dominions among his three sons. He begins
the document with a declaration that it is intended to
prevent quarrels among the sons concerning the limits
of their states; and then accurately defines the limits.
He does not in this division recognise anything like a

united France, a united Germany, or a united Italy.
The first division includes Aquitaine and Gascony, up
to the Loire ; and the south of modern France in
prolongation of the line of the Loire, Languedoc and
Provence, Savoy and Maurienne, and the parts of
Burgundy and Spain that fall within these lines—this
is given to Lewis. The second division, that of Pipin,
contains Lombardy and Bavaria ; Alemannia to the
south of the Danube, and the portions of what is now
Switzerland that fall between that and the inheritance
of Lewis. To Charles is left Austrasia, Saxony, the
north or Neustrian part of France, Thuringia and
Alemannia to the north of the Danube, and the rest
of Burgundy.   Each is to have a way by his own
territories into Italy, Lewis by the valley of Susa, Pipin
by the Noric or Tyrolese Alps, Charles by the valley
of Aosta—the French, Swiss, and German passes.
A further division is made in case of either brother's
death, and provision in case the nations should wish
to be governed by a son of the defunct.   Several
strict injunctions follow for perpetual peace between the
brothers, for the settlement of all disputes, for the
protection of the Church and Holy See, for the pre-
vention of the cruelties and oppressions amongst his
posterity by which he had seen competitors for the
throne disposed of amongst his predecessors. Of the
inheritance of the empire there is not a word. Was
it too sacred to be divided ? Or too hazardous to be
promised ? Or was not the bestowal of it to be decided
otherwise ? All was decided otherwise ; in 813 Charles,
seeing his two other sons dead and his own end
approaching, declared Lewis to be Emperor and King
after him. In 814 he died, and with him the strength
of the Franks. We learn from this that Charles, with

all his wisdom, did not foresee the natural division
of his empire which took place at a later period.
Perhaps he saw, more strongly than later ages, the
division between Northern and Southern France, and
Northern and Southern Germany ; anyhow, his division
is lateral rather than vertical, as was the later one
which prevailed under his grandsons, and more or
less throughout modern history.

The Organisation of Charles' Dominions.—As for the
lower organisation of the dominions of the Franks
under Charles, it is impossible to go into much detail
with much certainty. Most of the institutions of the
several German races have a strong family likeness :
the annual *placita*, or general conventions, once for
deliberation, and once for military demonstration ;
the administration of the provinces by dukes, appointed
from time to time by the king, and by their title
explaining that it was for the purposes of war that
they were first and chiefly appointed ; the subdivision
of the duchies into counties, with a count and his
assessors to administer justice and to account for
revenue ; the regulation of lay and ecclesiastical
assemblies, the *mallus* and the council, according to
the nature and extent of the jurisdiction of the pre-
siding officer ; the division of the countships into
hundreds and the jurisdiction of the *centenarius ;*—
all these are points in which the records of the Franks,
and of any other Teutonic nation, recall simply to
our minds the corresponding system among the Anglo-
Saxons : the ealdorman, and the sheriff and his thanes ;
the county court and the hundred court ; the jurisdiction of the bishop and the abbot. All these developments of the ancient German rule subsisted under
the several varieties of law. The wide dominions of

Charles embraced populations living under several systems of laws, several of them not German ; the Roman, the Visigoth, the Burgundian, had his own law, derived doubtless in one way or other from the Imperial Code. The Visigothic was a translation of or selection from the Theodosian Code ; the Roman was probably the Theodosian Code itself ; the Burgundian leavened more slightly. The Frank, the Saxon, the Alemannian, and the Bavarian had his own purer or more genuine German institution. Each man carried his law with him. Of course in Germany, where the population was purer, there were less chances of difficulty arising from such commixture, and the varieties of law were more distinctly local. Still the populations were so ruled, and not by a central legislation, although the central legislation was constantly being called in to amend or to add to the law. Throughout Germany, then, native law was still administered by native tribunals, in which the royal officers appointed to preside presided. There was, however, in the institution of the Missi Dominici, a distinct central jurisdiction, exercised by agents of the king, travelling through every province and bringing supreme justice within the reach of every freeman. Such in broad outline is the constitutional condition of the dominions of Charles the Great. The feudal system was further off in appearance than it was in time ; and it might seem that many and great changes must take place before the hereditary duchies and counties should take the place of imperial appointments, and the hereditary possession of land become a sign of subordination instead of freedom. The times were, however, rapid in movement, and before the century ends there are clear indications of the existence of the system, although as yet wanting in elaboration and consistency. The changes, geographical and successional, of the century of the Karolings will now be described, followed by a speculation on the actual rise of feudalism and its peculiarities in Germany.

The Reign of Lewis the Pious, 814–840 : *the Division of his Dominions.*—It is by the growth of feudalism that Germany, and the dependencies of the German sovereigns, became formed into an imperial whole, one and uniform in appearance, although wanting in real and lasting unity. The reign of Lewis the Pious began favourably enough : his sons were only boys ; he had three, a number on which Charles had congratulated himself in 806 ; and the eldest was but fifteen. The first measure of Lewis was to reconcile himself with the Saxons ; he received the homage of all the tributaries of the Franks, the adhesion of the Pope, and, two years after his accession to the empire, the imperial crown. Therewith began his troubles. He must proceed, as his father had, to a division of his dominions, but he was already hampered by the gift which Charles had made of Italy to his grandson Bernard. The division was published at Aix-la-Chapelle in 817 ; Lothair, the eldest son, was, after prayer and deliberation with fasting and almsgiving, chosen to be crowned and associated with his father in the imperial dignity ; Pipin and Lewis were to be kings, and, *sub seniore fratre*, to enjoy royal power under certain conditions after the father's death. A step is here taken, in advance of Charles' programme, by the provision of a constant central authority in the suzerain or emperor. The actual division is this : Pipin had Aquitaine, the march of Toulouse, one county in Languedoc, and three in Burgundy ; nearly the position which Lewis had himself received in 806. To Lewis is

given Bavaria, with all Germany to the east of Bavaria.
The rest is retained for the associated father and son,
and includes of course the whole northern half of what
then was Christian Europe. To the emperor (imperial
brother) every year the two kings were to pay a visit
and presents, to be accepted by him and returned with a
liberality proportioned to his superior power; to him
they were to look for aid in foreign wars; internal wars
were to be no longer possible; but such foreign wars
were not to be undertaken without his leave, although
they might receive messages of peace and friendship
without his interference. Provision is made for succession to the several portions, so that in case of death the
dominion shall not be further subdivided; a new king
out of the children of the defunct is to be chosen by the
people; if he leaves no children, his portion is to return
to the elder brother; the elder brother is to be guardian
of the realm in case of a minority. Italy is to go to the
elder brother on the father's death; by this we learn
that Bernard, to whom his grandfather had given Italy,
was in disgrace. He claimed, in fact, the right of empire
as his father's son; for this he was tried, condemned
to death, and blinded. He died three days after the
operation was performed, and so left the stage clear. It
will be seen that the theory of this division was to
preserve, with Germany and the imperial dignity, a
decided superiority to the elder brother, with some
semblance to what would later be called feudal supremacy. The two did not indeed hold their lands of him,
but they were obliged to recognise his suzerainty by
presents, whilst he retained the right of wardship and
escheat. By one clause, however, Lewis provides that
the vassal of each brother shall, after his own death,
hold his benefice in the power of his lord only; and

that those who had no lords should be allowed to commend themselves to which of the three they chose, and to possess their private or allodial lands according to their own native law. Such a plan as this has symmetry and much else to recommend it ; but it required less ambitious, less violent men to administer it. Nor would it bear much alteration ; a finger laid upon it would shake it ; the acquisition of new territory by any one of the brothers might upset the balance ; death or a new competitor might split up the whole amalgamation. And in point of fact so it was.

The Effect of the Birth of Charles the Bald, 823.—The result of the birth of a fourth son to Lewis, Charles, afterwards Charles the Bald, was such as to discredit for ever the second marriages of princes.[1] He was the

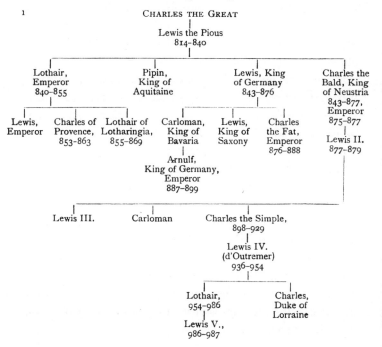

1

CHARLES THE GREAT
|
Lewis the Pious
814-840
|

Lothair, Emperor 840-855	Pipin, King of Aquitaine	Lewis, King of Germany 843-876	Charles the Bald, King of Neustria 843-877, Emperor 875-877
Lewis, Emperor	Charles of Provence, 853-863	Lothair of Lotharingia, 855-869	Carloman, King of Bavaria	Lewis, King of Saxony	Charles the Fat, Emperor 876-888	Lewis II. 877-879

Arnulf,
King of Germany,
Emperor
887-899

Lewis III.	Carloman	Charles the Simple, 898-929

Lewis IV.
(d'Outremer)
936-954

Lothair, 954-986	Charles, Duke of Lorraine

Lewis V.,
986-987

son of Lewis by Judith the daughter of Welf, the Lord
of Weingarten in Bavaria, and was born in 823. For
him his father very naturally wished to make provision, and tried to persuade Lothair to join in bestowing on him a part of the territory hitherto reserved.
Alemannia, with Rhaetia and part of Burgundy, *i.e.*
Swabia and modern Switzerland, were accordingly
allotted to him at a diet at Worms in 829, greatly to the
disgust of the other brothers. The immediate result
of this act was a rebellion, and the deposition of Lewis
the Pious from any share in the administration, a
measure which was forced on him by Pipin at Compiègne in the year following. But this arrangement
was short-lived. Lothair, who had consented to his
father's deposition, was forced to return to his obedience, and the measures of Pipin were reversed; for
the time Lothair was obliged to be content with the
kingdom of Italy. There was thus for a short period
a *fivefold* division. The father keeps North France
and North Germany, Pipin has South France, Charles
South-Western, and Lewis South-Eastern Germany.
But this was itself a short-lived arrangement; in 832
Pipin was disgraced, and Aquitaine was taken from
him and given to Charles. A new division was proposed between him and Lothair, and a new quarrel
followed. The Pope attempted in vain to mediate.
Lewis led an army to chastise the rebels, and was
deserted by them at the Lügenfeld (the field of lies),
between Basel and Strassburg. The great humiliation
of Lewis followed; he was now deposed from the
empire, deprived of the society of his wife and little
son, and condemned by the bishops to retire to a
monastery. Lothair was placed at the head of the
Frank empire, and is said to have meditated even the

death of his father. The supremacy of Lothair again
provoked a reaction in favour of Lewis. Lothair fled
before his brothers, Lewis was again released and re-
habilitated at S. Denys, and restored to his kingdoms.
He and Lothair met in arms before Blois, and the
son, seeing himself unequal to a battle, submitted.
The sons were then replaced in their estates and peace
followed. But hardly two years after, Lewis the father
provoked a new rebellion by proposing to associate
the little Charles in the imperial title and authority;
the brothers objected, and the project was for the
time frustrated—instead of the empire Charles being
invested with the kingdom of Neustria, Pipin consent-
ing. But a further division followed in 837, which
gave to Lothair the empire, Italy and the lands between
the Rhine and Meuse, with part of Burgundy; to Lewis
the son, besides Bavaria, Saxony and the other conquests of his grandfather; to Pipin, Aquitaine and
Neustria; to Charles, Burgundy and Franconia. To
this division Lewis the son demurred; he wanted the
whole of Germany, and to gain it he took up arms
and held out against his father for two years.

Death of the Emperor Lewis : the Division of Verdun,
843.—Just at the moment that the father was expecting
to mediate between the conflicting brothers, he died.
Pipin had died two years before him, and Charles had
then entered upon Aquitaine. The division of the
empire had thus become very nearly what was afterwards arranged : modern France was held by Charles ;
Lewis had the most of Germany ; Lothair the intermediate territory and Italy, with imperial supremacy.
Into the minutiæ of the quarrels which occupied the
three following years it is almost impossible to go ;
Lothair attempted, by using one brother against the

other, to get the reality of imperial authority into his hands; Lewis took the opportunity of securing the allegiance of the whole of the German provinces; after several other combinations, the three brothers met and fought at Fontenai on the 25th of June 841. Lothair was beaten. For two years more he struggled on with great pertinacity and incurable bad faith, and at last, in August 843, at Verdun, the final division took place. Lewis at last got the whole of Germany to the east of the Rhine, with several cities on the west of the Rhine to provide him with wine; Charles had France to the west of the Meuse and Rhone; Lothair had Italy, the name of emperor, and the intervening territory, which had once been Ripuarian France, the duchy on the Mosel, Burgundy and Provence, which in the Karoling times was called, after either him or after his son of the same name who succeeded to it, Lotharingia or Lorraine, including what was later the county or kingdom of Burgundy and the kingdom of Arles, and later still the inheritance and conquests of Charles the Bold and the county of Provence, and later still the Austrian Netherlands (the plunder ground of Lewis XIV.), the whole including what is now Belgium and the east of France down to the Mediterranean.

Its Importance.—The great importance of the division of Verdun is the fact that it set Germany free from the rest of the Frank empire, for the three sons of Lewis were henceforth equals; Lothair remained emperor, but the imperial title involved no supremacy. From this point the administration of public law and constitutional history in Germany begins. The Germany of Lewis the German comprised Bavaria with all the territory to the East—Alemannia, Franconia, Saxony, and Thuringia.

The Rhine for the greatest part of its course was the boundary between him and Lothair, and in the north, where the Rhine was not the limit, a line drawn from the mouth of the Weser to the Rhine, where it takes a bend a little below Coblenz. To this division of Friesland we are to attribute the fact that the present kingdom of Holland, the only German-speaking land beside England, was not included in Germany, nor, whilst Germany and the empire were nearly conterminous, in the empire itself, although belonging to the person who was emperor; nor, after the empire expired, was it included in the Germanic Confederation which ended in 1866. It remains perhaps for us to see whether it may not yet be swallowed up in a Prussianised Germany.[1]

It is almost impossible to retain these details in the memory, but the effect of an attempt to do so ought to enable the historian to realise more thoroughly than any other process the actual continuance of the old national limits within this constantly changing aggregate of empire. Although held by different brothers and in different combinations, Alemannia, Saxony, Bavaria, Franconia, Hessia, Thuringia, Meissen, and Lausitz preserve their identity and continue to preserve it, with their nationality, their own laws, and the characteristic ecclesiastical differences which have from the first distinguished them. Further, we ought to try to gather from the details the impression of the pertinacious and foreseeing policy of Lewis, well called the German, who from the beginning of his father's reign was in possession of Bavaria, and bent on gradually annexing all the German conquests of Charles the Great. We see that he finally succeeded in doing so, and so doing

---

[1] This remark, made many years ago (in 1868), is well worthy of notice.

separating them for ever from the kingdom which retained the name of the Franks. Henceforth Germany rapidly ceases to be Frank at all.

The Reign of Lewis the German, 843–876.—Lewis the German reigned a long time, thirty-three years after the peace of Verdun; he lost no part of his estates, and acquired nothing from Lothair or Charles. He laboured hard to extend his dominions eastwards; in 844 he conquered the Obotrites, in modern Mecklenburg; in 848 he humbled the Bohemians, although he was defeated by them the next year; and in 855 he was unsuccessful against the Slavs, though after that year his fortune seems to have looked up, and he not only defended but extended the eastern frontier. The northern boundary of the Eyder also he managed to preserve. But he was not spared the fate of his family, his sons, by their jealousies and demands of estates, being a source of constant difficulty to him. His career, however, is a marked contrast to that of his brothers Lothair and Charles, and on the whole there seems to have been either in his conduct or in his character more that redeems him in the eyes of the historians. Although not a missionary king like Charles, he did a great deal for the promotion of learning and religion amongst his more civilised subjects, and left a good report behind him. He died in 876, leaving three sons—Carloman, King of Bavaria (880); Lewis II., King of Saxony (882); and Charles the Fat, King of Alemannia, the last becoming afterwards also emperor (876–888) and possessor nominally of all the lands of the Franks. Of these sons Carloman survived him four years, succeeded to Italy on the death of his uncle Charles the Bald, and died in 880. Lewis succeeded in 877 to Lorraine, and, on the death of Carloman, to Bavaria, but survived him only two years, dying in 882. Charles the Fat succeeded in 879 to the empire; in 880 to Italy; in 882 to Bavaria and Saxony; in 884 to France and Burgundy. But he was not a man of any real power, nor were the Germans willing to be again lost in the empire of a nominal prince. Carloman, the popular son of Lewis the German, had left a bastard, Arnulf, Duke of Carinthia, who headed a confederacy against Charles the Fat, who was deposed at Tribur in 887 when Arnulf was created King of Germany. The French had been very shy of acknowledging Charles the Fat; he does not count amongst their Charleses at all. Losing Germany he lost all the real power he had; he died the next year, 888. With the succession of Arnulf we must begin a new period.

Feudalism.—Attention must now be directed to the process which underlies all this chopping and changing; the development of feudalism and the feudalising of Germany. Unfortunately the growth of feudalism has been treated generally far more in reference to French than to German history: the French, with their great power of definition and organisation, have imparted to the growth of the system a hardness of outline which it did not possess, and which of course approaches the truth more nearly in France than elsewhere; which is therefore inapplicable generally to the history of England and Germany. In some measure this may be justified by the fact that feudalism was an especially Frank system, and was really carried out more definitely in France than elsewhere. Still it is a misfortune that we have no more definite account of its growth in Germany also. Feudalism, I need hardly tell you, is that system of mutual interdependence between lord and vassal, depending on the holding of land, and binding the whole body politic in a system of close gradations, the vassal holding his land of, doing his duty to, and expecting protection from his immediate lord, who is in the same relation to another until the social pyramid is crowned by royalty. The system in theory originates in the conquest of a kingdom, which is parted out by the king or general amongst his followers, who hold their shares of him by military service, and subdivide that share to their followers in turn on similar or lower services. Practically it has not grown up under such conditions, except perhaps in England after the Conquest by the Normans, when the law was to some extent accommodated to the theory; and in the Frank colonies of the Crusades, where it was pure and simple. Certainly in the Frank Empire it grew up otherwise, for it sprang not out of a general division of the kingdom, but from a gradual concretion and assimilation of different territories and different characters in their owners.

Stages in the Growth of Feudalism.—The first stage of such feudalism was of course the bestowal of an estate by way of provision on a faithful servant or an important minister; which involved the performance of certain duties generally if not always military, and was termed *beneficium;* the second step was for the beneficium to become hereditary; and the third was as soon as hereditary succession gave the means of ensuring a perfect title, when the beneficiary was allowed to carve out minor holdings, for his own dependants, to be held by similar services. But even after this had been done two great points remained to be added. First the universalising of the system, so that all states should be held on feudal tenure; and secondly, the joining to the feudal ownership such rights of actual jurisdiction as made the large beneficiary sovereign over his feudal dependants, except so far as the authority of his own superior entered in. The first of these points, the spreading of feudalism over the whole of a country, was attained by the process of commendation, according to which the small independent landowners were constantly putting themselves under the protection of one neighbour lord for and against another, and as a condition of that dependence, granting him a feudal hold on the land which was hitherto all their own. This process had largely prevailed in England before the Norman Conquest, though without actual mention of feudality. But in France it spread probably with more rapidity and covered the whole country. The second point, the conjunction of hereditary magistracy with feudal possession, can only have sprung from the union of the office of imperial governor with the ownership of great lands in the province of which the government was so held. As the benefice became hereditary, so the magistracy might also follow suit, and then as the central power became weaker and the feudatory more powerful at home, the authority which had been delegated would become inherent, and so either exclude the superior jurisdiction of the suzerain or make it impossible to exercise it until every provincial count or duke was really sovereign in his own duchy or county. It is well known how this did result in France and how from Charles the Bald to Lewis IX. France was full of kings, amongst whom the real sovereign was often the weakest and had less territory than many of his nobles.

Illustrations from French and German History.—The greatest part of French history, down to the end of

Lewis IX.'s reign, is taken up with the succession to, the absorption of, and emission of these great fiefs from the demesnes of the owner, whilst the efforts of the feudatories to maintain their several privileges quite puts out of sight the existence of anything like the ancient machinery of national unity. Private war, private alliances, private courts of injustice, private coinage and the exclusion of royal jurisdiction, are the subjects of the constitutional history of France. With Germany, however, it was very much the reverse, although the actual result of subdivision was the same, and owing to the position of the two countries at the close of the Middle Ages, is even now historically clearer in Germany than in France. This will form a leading topic in most of the ensuing chapters; and the more detailed view even of the theory of German feudalism must now be left to the next chapter. It is only necessary here to remark that the differences in Germany arose from the greater extent of power left in the hands of native allodial owners, often the descendants of the old hereditary rulers of the provinces; secondly, from the greater strength of the central power, a source of strength as well as of weakness being the title of the empire, both Roman and Frank; and thirdly, from the greater force of disruption resulting from the removal of the greater force of cohesion. Both in France and Germany feudalism grew, owing to the necessities of the same time, the time of the dissensions of the Karolingian house; but in France the royal power, at first infinitesimal, is seen growing and strengthening from Hugh Capet to Lewis XI.; in Germany what was a strong central force at first, made stronger by adjunction to the empire, is seen breaking up in the misfortunes of Frederick II., and at once proceeding to a thorough and still working disruption of elements never from the first thoroughly amalgamated.

IMPORTANT DATES

Coronation of Charles the Great as Emperor, 800.
Death of Charles the Great, 814.
Reign of Lewis the Pious, 816–840.
Treaty of Verdun, 843.
Reign of Lewis I. the German, 843–876.
Death of Charles the Fat (King, 876–888 ; Emperor, 880–888), 888.

CHAPTER IV

Feudalism in Germany.—There are many points in the history of feudalism, as exemplified in Germany, which would be interesting if we were now investigating the customs and jurisprudence of that country. In this chapter, however, only such particulars will be adduced as throw light upon the process by which Germany passed from being a geographical expression for a group of kindred but independent nations, to be a consolidated kingdom under a central authority, and how from being a kingdom consolidated under central authority, it became a confederation of almost independent states bound together by an elective head, whose power and authority rested more on his own personal influence than on the endowments or prerogatives of his official position. By the conquest of Charles the Great, and by the uniform policy of the long reign of Lewis the German, Germany had become one state, and one with well-defined limits ; and that consolidation survived the line of its creators, short as it may have been. Charles the Fat was deposed and perished twelve years after the death of his father, and his German kingdom bestowed itself with one consent on the son of his brother Carloman, Arnulf, Duke of Carinthia, the last

German king of the line of the Great Charles. But although Arnulf was a son of Carloman, he was the son of a concubine, and he succeeded by the election of the subjects of Charles not by virtue of any family compact. The very succession is a proof of the change which already prevailed in a feudal direction, that the barons of Germany so lately the Antrustiones, the beneficiaries or officials of Frankish kings, were now able to command the election of their own master. But the change is really not so great as it seems : the right of choosing a king on a vacancy from the members of the royal house was primitive among the German nations ; and it was expressly provided for in the settlement by Charles in the year 806 that, if either of his younger sons should die, the people of the kingdom he had ruled might choose, if they liked, one of his sons to reign over them in preference to the surviving uncles. Bastardy counted for little in those days, as we see from the succession of Bernard in Italy ; and Arnulf was the recognised son of Carloman, the eldest son of Lewis the German.

Characteristics of Feudalism : (1) *In Germany.*—Before summing up the reigns that intervene between the end of the Karolings and the institution of the Saxon line, in which was restored the empire to Germany in the person of Otto I., it is advisable to amplify what has been already written about feudalism in Germany. (1) The fact that Germany, although a conquered country, was conquered by a kindred race, and that the wisest monarchs of that race were content with the acquiescence of the conquered nations in their religion and government, without insisting on a reappointment of their lands or repudiation of their ancient laws, but admitted them at once, or very shortly after their sub-

jugation, into an equality of position with their conquerors, had the effect of continuing a large portion
of the land of the conquered countries in the same
allodial tenure on which it was held before the conquest. Feudal tenure was not a fundamental principle
of the Frank system, nor indeed was the feudal principle
as yet so fully developed, and to feudalise the whole of
Germany would have required an extent and a disper-
sion of Frank nobility which, if possible, would have
been dangerous. The result of this was the leaving
allodial estates of considerable extent, which continue
to subsist in the heirs of the ancient indigenous nobility,
and whose tenure was unaffected by ever so large an
admixture with properties feudally held, or as it became
the fashion to call them on the principles of the civil
law, *fidei commissa*. The existence of an indigenous
allodial nobility has of course an enormous effect in
the maintenance of national or provincial feeling. Still
more is this the case when, in the distribution of
imperial offices, magistracies, or provincial governor-
ships, accompanied by large beneficiary provision, were
given to the leading nobles of the old stock. Such gifts
would, having once become attached to an ancient
national house, have a tendency to become hereditary,
and having become hereditary, would have the strongest
possible chance of being lasting ; for the basis of their
duration lying in the good government they could carry
out, they would have the firmest support in the affection
of those under their charge ; the supreme power, if
above jealousy, being thankful to the house that proved
its faith by its wise government. Hence, if it is found,
for instance, that in Saxony large estates were retained
by their ancient owners on an unaltered tenure, and
that the emperors or kings were wise enough to fill

the magistracies with these and bestow on them the provision meet for such a position, it may be taken as certain that it will not be long before the Saxon dukedom becomes hereditary, and that under hereditary dukes it will continue, perhaps indeed faithful to the general interest of the empire of which it forms a part, and far more certainly as national or as provincial in spirit as it was before, or even perhaps more so.

(2) *In France.*—With France it was not so. Owing to the fact that the old Gauls were an alien people from the Frank conquerors, and civilised under a law of their own, much less amalgamation took place ; the conquerors retained their character of a superior race and the land was more thoroughly subject to a feudal tenure, the overlordship passing entirely to Franks. Thus the Frank provincial governors, who afterwards developed into the great feudatories, were less of national or provincial princes than the German, were more definitely provided for by feudal benefices, were more dependent on the maintenance of their feudal position, were less likely to recover power after once having lost it, but were more likely to become speedily and uninterruptedly hereditary. If they lost their benefices, their feudal estates, they were nothing ; but the German allodial lord, even if he lost his imperial office, could fall back on his own ancestral one. Hence with a strong tendency in the German counts and dukes to become hereditary, and to maintain hereditary houses from which their successors could be taken, there was a much greater tendency in the French nobles to retain consecutive hold of power. Thus whilst the early portion of the tenth century is the period at which dukedoms and counties in France became hereditary, in Germany in spite of the tendency, it is not until

the eleventh. It is not to be forgotten, however, that in France the Franks had been established since the sixth, whilst in Germany the old national divisions had subsisted almost in integrity until the ninth century.

The Royal Power in France and Germany.—Taking these things together it is not difficult to see that the central authority, the supreme king, will retain his power longer, and also that the general assembly of the estates of his kingdom will continue to be a substantive power in the empire much longer, where the great provincial dignities have not become permanently hereditary, and yet a provincial nobility has grown into hereditary wealth and strength. In France where the feudalism was complete, the assembly of estates was little else than a collection of minor feudatories under the direction of their overlords, lay or ecclesiastical ; they were faithful, or could not help being faithful, to their hereditary counts, and if the hereditary counts were strong enough to keep them faithful they were strong enough to coerce the king. This they did. They reduced him to a nonentity, and might have set him aside without finding the want of him. In Germany, however, the king could always look for support in a diet of the estates, which contained an element of independent hereditary nobility, not dependent on the dukes or counts ; in which the dukes or counts were still nominated not yet hereditary, and the office therefore a matter for competition among the faithful nobles ; and, even where it had become hereditary, there would always be a strong independent party to support the central power against the subordinates. And so it was. Very much as in England before the Norman Conquest, the earldoms were tending to become hereditary but were not yet so ; there was an abundant aristocracy able and willing to claim them when they became vacant; but the king could depend on the resolution of the Witenagemote when it became necessary to remove or to punish any of them, and there was no fear of the king sharing the fate of his fellow in France. Of course, as has already been said, the removal of the central pressure would have a much greater tendency to produce disruption in Germany than in France.

France and Germany in the Tenth Century.—These reasons account for the difference between the histories of Germany and France in the Middle Ages. At the point now reached France was falling rapidly, had in fact nearly fallen into the hands of the great counts and dukes whose successors, and often their descendants, portioned it out among themselves for several centuries, until Philip II. by lying and chicanery, and Lewis IX. by wise marriages and honest policy, managed to recover most of the great fiefs and vest them in members of the royal house. In this very year, 887, at the time of the deposition of Charles the Fat from the throne of Germany at Tribur, he was deposed from that of France, and Eudes, Count of Paris, was chosen king. Here was at once a vassal who had succeeded his father and left his inheritance to his brother, in the county of Paris and duchy of France. In Germany the time was not yet ripe for the choosing of a mere vassal ; but, when it does come, it will be seen that the choice fell on a noble whose position is by no means so well ascertained, but who practised the rule, which long continued in force, of immediately devolving his former dignities upon another prince.

The Close of the Reign of Charles the Fat, Emperor 880–888, *and King of France* 884–887.—It is now necessary to return to Charles the Fat.[1] For three years we see this unfortunate prince at the head of all the possessions of his house. The great line of the Karolings being now reduced to himself, a childless man, and the little Charles, son of Lewis the Stammerer, with hereditary claims on the throne of France, but now only five years old. The misfortunes of Charles the Fat came upon him suddenly and overwhelmingly; he lost all powers of body and mind by disease; the deposition of him in 887 was a matter of necessity, but it was carried out with, it would seem, unnecessary barbarity. If he was diseased and idiotic or even raving mad, there was no reason why he should be deprived of the necessaries of life and left as pensioner to the charity of a bishop. His death, which occurred in 888, was attributed to strangulation; and, as there is no reason to imagine that Arnulf would have been unnecessarily cruel, or that it was the interest of any one else to get rid of him, it is perhaps most reasonable to suppose that he was put out of the way as an unmanageable and dangerous madman. He died at Indingen in his own Alemannian kingdom, and was buried at Richenau near Constance.

The Karoling States.—Of the other Karoling States little need be said. France became the ground of contention between Charles the Simple and his house, and the Counts of Paris who finally supplanted them. Italy fell into the hands for many years of its own nobles, who elected themselves kings and emperors at Roncaglia, until Otto of Saxony in the following century recovered the empire; to this period belong the emperors Guy and Lambert of Spoleto, Berengar of

---

[1] From 876 to 879 Charles the Fat reigned along with his brothers Carloman and Lewis. On their deaths he reigned alone.

Friuli, Hugh of Arles, Berenger of Tuscany, and the rest who puzzle the student by their insignificance and contemporaneousness. Italy was indeed a battle ground for the rival families, who, out of its own bounds, thought themselves entitled to its sovereignty. It was a debatable ground for competitors from all the other kingdoms.

Lotharingia.—But, if the history of Italy at this period is confusing, still more is that of Lotharingia, the kingdom of the Lothairs, that lay between France and Germany and the stock of whose rulers was quite worn out. The failure of Charles the Fat in 888 was remedied by an election in France and Germany; but in Lotharingia it was the signal for a break-up. The territory had no natural unity and never fell again really under one sceptre, until the time of Napoleon I. Several subdivisions of Lotharingia under the sons and nephews of Lothair I. had helped the process of disintegration, but it had been nominally united under Charles the Fat, and for the last time. Boso, King of Provence, who had some sort of claim by the gift of Carloman of Bavaria, maintained himself in his portion of Lotharingia and left it to his son. Transjurane Burgundy erected itself into a kingdom for Rudolf, a son of Conrad, Count of Auxerre, whose successor Rudolf II. united the kingdom of Provence with his own and called himself King of Arles; the crown descended in his posterity until it was bequeathed by Rudolf III. to Conrad the Salic king and emperor in 1032. The northern half of Lotharingia retained the title of Lorraine, but it also broke up into Upper and Lower. It still remained nominally subject to Germany, and came with Germany to Arnulf, who made it a kingdom for his son Zwentibold; on his misbehaviour the Lorrainers chose his brother Lewis, and on his death Charles the Simple. It soon after, in 959, fell under the sovereignty of its dukes, who had been hitherto beneficiary only. Otto gave Lower Lorraine to Godfrey I. and Upper Lorraine to Frederick, Count of Bar; from thenceforth, although occasionally personally united, they became permanently divided; the last remnant of the Karolings wore themselves out in Lower Lorraine, and Upper Lorraine became a hereditary dukedom of no great importance to German history. It is important, however, to observe that Lotharingia continues to be, in its integrity or in its disruption, feudally a part of the Germany which in the next century was to reconstitute the empire.

Arnulf, King 887–889, *and Emperor* 894, *and his son Lewis* 900–911.—Arnulf[1] was elected King of Germany in 887 at Tribur; subject to his approval Eudes was elected King of France; Berengar, one of the competitive kings of Italy, made him his protector. He followed up for the most part the policy of his grandfather in attempting to humiliate the Slav nations on the eastern frontier, and he conquered the Moravians; but he also fought the Normans and drove them out of the Low Countries. In 893 he recovered Lorraine and gave it to his son Zwentibold; by his management Charles the Simple received the crown of France; he himself at length entered the lists for the empire and was crowned by Pope Formosus in 896. His character does not strike us very forcibly; but there was no doubt considerable power about the man, probably of

---

[1] Arnulf, the successor of Charles the Fat in Germany, was the illegitimate son of Carloman, brother of Charles.

the same sort as his grandfather Lewis the German had possessed. He reigned three years after he took the imperial title, and was kept constantly on the move between Bavaria and Italy. He died in 899, or, as some writers say, 900; his legitimate children were the child Lewis, who succeeded him, and two daughters :— Hedwige, whom he married to Otto the Great, Duke of Saxony, the father of Henry the Fowler, and Glismond, who married Conrad of Fritzlar, Count of Franconia, and was mother of Conrad I., King of Germany. His son Lewis, often known as Lewis the Child, succeeded him as King of Germany at seven years old, and soon afterwards he was received as King of Lorraine. He was placed under the government of Otto of Saxony, his brother-in-law, and Archbishop Hatto of Mainz. His great war was with the Hungarians, by whom he was defeated, and who now begin to bear an important part in German history; this defeat seems to have broken his heart, for he died in 911 and left no children. His cousin Charles the Simple was too contemptible, it would seem, to be accepted as his successor, and we close with him the record of the fortunes of the Frank kings of Germany. Henceforth we find ourselves in the midst of a new set of actors of whom an account will now be given.

The Hungarians.—And first of all, who were these Hungarians who defeated Lewis ? Just at the same moment the Frank kingdoms were assailed on the west and on the east; on the west by the Normans, on the east by the Hungarians, or Magyars. How the Normans were bribed by Charles the Simple with the gift of Normandy, and how they gradually were Christianised into Crusaders and civilised into French

speaking before they conquered England, we learn
from French and English history. But of the Hungarians we know little comparatively, but that they
were a Tartar tribe, known in their own tongue as
Magyar ; they were a fierce tribe of hunters and fisher-
men, and they drove with them enormous herds of
sheep and oxen. For a picture of their march, a
little perhaps indebted to fancy, the 55th chapter of
Gibbon must be consulted. The historians have not
ventured to give a date for the beginning of their
wanderings, but relate that they started from the
country on the west side of the Chinese wall, and
partly conquering before them, and impelled by other
barbarous tribes, especially the Patzinaks behind them,
reached Pannonia, then a Slavonian country and
nominally subject to the empire, about fifteen years
before the end of the ninth century. The date of
their entering Germany is well fixed, it is the year 890.
Just then Arnulf was sore pressed by the Normans
and was engaged in a war with the Moravian chieftain
to whom he had just given Bohemia. Unhappily forgetful of the example of the Lombards, he invited the
Magyars to his help and with their aid succeeded in
humbling the Slavs ; but the step was fatal, and for a
hundred years these Magyars or Huns, as they were
called, desolated Germany, destroyed the cities as far
north as Bremen and as far south as Pavia, whilst
towards the west they reached the Rhine in the reign
of Lewis. During Arnulf's reign they rested, but with
Lewis their aggressions began ; they invaded South
Germany, met him at a place called Ansburg, and broke
his young spirit by the defeat. As Gog and Magog, the
astonished Germans regarded them as the forerunners

of Antichrist, and of that end of the world which was to come in the year 1000. Happily the year, although it did not see the end of the world, saw the end of their barbarism; for in the year 997 Stephen their leader was converted and baptized, whilst, in the year of destiny, he was received into the number of Christian kings with the special title of Apostle or Apostolic Majesty.

Otto of Saxony and Conrad of Franconia.—Such was the cloud which hung over Germany when Lewis, the last of the Karolings, died. The crisis was one which demanded a general, or rather a dictator; it was no time for balancing equivalent claims, or enduring weakness for the sake of an hereditary title. Charles the Simple had to surrender Normandy the very year that Lewis died. But who were the men, and what were the relations among themselves, from whom a saviour of the fallen kingdom could be chosen? Fortunately there were two men whose character fitted them for the position, and who had both greatness of mind not to begrudge it to the other. These were Otto, Duke of Saxony, the brother-in-law, and Conrad, Duke of Franconia, the nephew of the late king. The constant chopping and changing of the divisions of Germany among the Karolings had had the effect of preserving the definiteness of the boundaries of the old nations; whilst the decline in personal importance of the kings had greatly increased the power of the officers, the governors, beneficiaries, dukes or counts who were set over them, and who sometimes added ancient independent claims to the delegated authority. In Saxony, Otto, the son of Ludolph, was believed among the Saxons to be a descendant of their ancient princes.

Ludolph was the son of Egbert, and his mother Ida, who was a canonised saint, was a daughter of the Duke Dietrich who had held out against the Great Charles. Other genealogies gave him Witikind as an ancestor. He was a Saxon prince, and was the third of his house who had held the office of duke or imperial lieutenant. Nowhere was the patriotic feeling so strong as in Saxony, consequently Otto was a thoroughly strong, powerful man; and he had exercised very great influence under both Arnulf and Lewis. But he was now growing old. The other prince, Conrad, Duke of Franconia, was, as you would naturally expect, a Frank probably by extraction; his father's name was Conrad, and it was rumoured that he was akin to the Karolings themselves, but the obscurity of the rise of the family seems fatal to any pretension of high nobility. His father Conrad, however, had been a very powerful man under Arnulf. His history illustrates the unsettled state of Franconia, under the administration of its imperial duke.[1] He by whatever title, and his three brothers, formed a design of conquering the Count of Bamberg, Adalbert, a nephew of Otto. They besieged him and a brother perished on one side : on the other side two, the brothers of Adalbert. The blood feud continued for several years, during which Conrad became Duke of Thuringia. It ended with his death in 905 or 907 in battle against Adalbert. The latter was persuaded by Archbishop Hatto to surrender, and was beheaded by Lewis. The example shows that private war, one of the essential evils of a feudal government, was an under-

---

[1] Lewis, King of Franconia, son of Lewis the German, died 882; and Franconia was divided between Adalbert of Bamberg and the imperial Duke Conrad.

stood practice; it also shows that Franconia,[1] in which Bamberg is so important a portion, was in a condition of very little permanent consolidation.

Bavaria, Swabia, and Alsace. — In fact, here as in France, under the influence of the earlier Frank possession, it is natural to expect to find feudalism more widely and early developed. Conrad the father may safely be called the founder of the house of Franconia; and Adalbert, who is called a nephew of the Duke of Saxony, may be considered to have been a competitor for the duchy. Bavaria was only now emerging from the state of subjection to movable governors, under a duke named Leopold, who, from the office of guardian of the Bavarian marches, had risen an important step; his origin is obscure, and he himself was not a likely man to be chosen. Of Swabia very little is known at

---

[1] Franconia, on the death of Lewis (King of Saxony and Franconia, son of Lewis the German) in 876, fell between the *Duke* Conrad and Adalbert, Count of Bamberg.

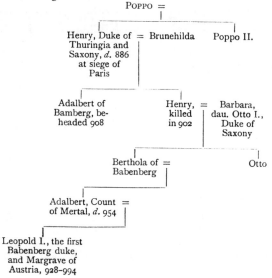

this period.   The duchy of Alemannia had been a good
deal pulled about during the decline of the Karolings.
Alsace had been made a duchy for Hugo, son of Lothair
II., and perhaps then detached from Swabia.   The
Swabian house from which the later emperors came,
sprang up in the eleventh century ; and, although a duchy
of Swabia was reconstituted by Henry the Fowler, none
of the houses which held it were long lived, and the
list of beneficiary dukes continues there longer than
elsewhere.

Election of Conrad as King, 911.—There is no exact
contemporary account of the election of emperor ; but
it seems certain that a general assembly of the German
nations took place, and that unanimously the throne was
offered to Duke Otto ; that Otto excused himself on
the ground of age and proposed his nephew Conrad.
Conrad was accepted and crowned.   The fact that the
Franks and Saxons alone are mentioned as taking part
in this transaction by the contemporary historians, has
led to a question whether the Bavarians and Alemanni
really took part in it.   It seems probable that the Franconians and Saxons only were represented in it by men
of much mark, who added like Otto and Conrad high
nobility to high office.   By such men neither Bavaria
nor Alemannia could force herself into a foremost place ;
but it would appear from the words of Witikind of
Corvey, that the election was *per cunctos populos*, that
it was at least formally carried out.   Conrad's character
fully justified the choice, in which Duke Otto had over-
looked the claims of his own children.   Clearly Conrad's
prospects of strong government depended much on
Otto's life.

Conrad's Reign and Difficulties, 911-919.—Otto died the
year after the election, and the king found himself in

immediate difficulties. The five nations over which he was called to rule in turn opposed themselves to him as rebels. They were, of course, the Saxons, Bavarians, Alemanni, Franconians, and to them have now to be added the Lorrainers. The quarrel with the Saxons began only too naturally on the death of Otto. Henry (called by later writers "the Fowler"), his son and Conrad's cousin, claimed, or took possession without claim, of his father's honours and estates. Conrad fearing his youth, it is said, but quite as probably fearing his power, did not admit him to the whole of the benefice possessed by his father, *i.e.* he either diminished his official estate, or diminished his official power; it is not certain which. But it is certain that Henry and his Saxons took umbrage at the treatment and rose in arms. Eberhard, Duke of Franconia, to whom Conrad had delivered over his duchy when he accepted the empire, was sent with an army into Saxony, and besieged Henry. Eberhard, deceived by a stratagem, retired from Saxony without any result, and Henry continued practically independent during the rest of the reign. In 913 Erchanger, Count of Alemannia or Alsace, rebelled, but the war was prevented by the marriage of Conrad with his sister. In the following year Erchanger rebelled again and was exiled. On attempting again to claim the authority of a duke, he was condemned to death as a traitor at Mainz in a Diet, and beheaded. His duchy was given to Burchard, who, possessing the government of Swabia also, bore the title of Duke of Alemannia in full right. He is in fact said to be the first Duke of Alemannia or Swabia, under the new kingdom. Encouraged by these difficulties of the king, Arnulf, Duke of Bavaria, who was nephew of Erchanger of Alsace, and had been active and successful in defending the frontiers against the

Hungarians, attempted to raise himself to the rank of an independent prince, but his fall was as signal as that of Erchanger. He fled to his old enemies the Hungarians, and invited them into Germany as his allies. These dreadful barbarians had not been at rest during the struggle in Saxony; they annually invaded Germany, taking a different route each year. In 912 they ravaged Thuringia and Franconia, in 913 Bavaria, in 915 and 916 Alemannia, Thuringia, and Saxony. In 917 they penetrated as far as Lorraine. In the valley of the Inn, a land fatal to invaders, they were defeated, but there only. In 919 Conrad went into Bavaria against Arnulf and his new allies; in the expedition he received a wound which ended in his death. Returning to Germany he called together the princes and recommended them to choose Henry, Duke of Saxony and Thuringia, as his successor. Shortly after this he died.

The Importance of Conrad's Reign.—The place occupied by this short reign is sufficiently definite, so definite in fact that on this probability a school of German jurists founded a theory, according to which Conrad reduced the whole of his dominions to a feudal symmetry; it was even held that the several dukes offered to hold their lands of Conrad in fee, and acquired the rights of sovereigns each in his own duchy. But this idea is rejected by the later scholars, and it seems better to regard the reign as a period, from which the causes which had been long at work begin to show their results more plainly. So viewed, it is the time at which the hereditary principle begins to oust the principle of nomination, except where the hereditary succession itself fails; and so henceforth the princes are rather vassals of the empire than its ministers. Certainly this is the case in Saxony, Franconia, and Bavaria; that it is not so in Lorraine and Alemannia is due rather to other circumstances such as have been described. It cannot be denied that in this matter Conrad sacrificed somewhat of the shadow of power for the reality; and although humbled by the success with which Henry the Fowler vindicated his independence in Saxony, gained by having him for a friend instead of a foe. But he did not proceed in the same way in Alemannia, where Erchanger paid the penalty of his great designs with his head; nor in Bavaria, where Arnulf was banished and exiled. But the reign of Conrad is too short to reveal much of his individual character, and the recommendation of Henry the Fowler for king must be set against the story which accuses Conrad of having sought to take his life. It is convenient to take this for an epoch, to which character perhaps there is little else to entitle it than that it comes between two great dynasties of distinctly different origin and policy, both of which bore the imperial title, and made it respected throughout the world. But to make it a period either of pure feudalism or even of distinct transition to feudalism is a mistake. Still more so would it be to suppose that the feudal idea was so rooted in Germany that the extinction of the Karolings involved the rise of their vassals to the rank of independent princes. Although it was certainly the object of the dukes to become kings, as they had seen the Karolings themselves kings of each one of the nations out of which the kingdom of Lewis the German had been composed, it would be to antedate the feudal idea far too much if we were to suppose that these men would have regarded the extinction of the house of the suzerain as a release from allegiance. It would be wiser to go back for a cause to the ancient national identity of the several nations, which is certainly seen in the Saxons and Bavarians, and in a less degree in the Franks. But it is more likely that Henry and Arnulf and Erchanger looked on themselves as candidates for the succession to Saxony, Bavaria, and Alemannia, as so many distinct thrones left open by the extinction of Karoling occupants, than as vacant by the conquest of Thassiloor or of Witikind. There was a time when Charles the Fat had been King of Franconia, Lewis of Saxony, Carloman of Bavaria, with no overlord. The imperial authority of the senior Karoling had been abolished at Verdun, and, although Arnulf was both King of Germany and emperor, the tie between the two characters was not yet drawn close ; Germany could do without either an emperor or a single king. The next period, that of the dominion of the Saxon house, which in its own representatives reconciled for one of the great divisions of the empire the substance and show of power, put an end for many centuries to the idea of dividing Germany into the old petty kingdoms. Bavaria and Saxony, although kept apart by jealousies and antipathies, do not come out as distinct monarchies until in the eighteenth century Prussia, and in the nineteenth Hanover, Bavaria, and Würtemberg, realised the dreams of the Bavarian Arnulf on the extinction of the Holy Roman Empire.

The Saxon Emperors.—The Saxon emperors are all men who vindicate their place in history by personal character. Hitherto we have watched the play of events with little knowledge of the lives or idiosyncrasies of the actors. Except the great Charles we have very indistinct conceptions of the Frank rulers ; of Lewis the Pious we know more perhaps than of the younger ones ; but the men for whom, whilst at the head of enormous territories, their subjects could find no better names than the Bald, the Stammerer, the

Fat, and the Simple, were perhaps more likely to leave a mark in history by their misfortunes and failures than by any origination of history by themselves. From this time we shall be able to trace the minds and working of great men for nearly three centuries of troubled but not obscured splendour.

IMPORTANT DATES

Accession of Arnulf (king and emperor), 887.
Deposition of Charles the Fat, 887.
Eudes (Odo), Count of Paris, becomes King of France, 887.
Defeat of the Northmen by Arnulf, 891.
Arnulf takes Rome, and is crowned Emperor, 894–896.
Charles the Simple succeeds Eudes, 898.
Arnulf is succeeded by his son, Lewis III., 899.
Reign of Lewis III., 899–911.
Reign of Conrad I. (of Franconia), 911–918.
Treaty of Clair-sur-Epte, 911.

CHAPTER V

The Reign of Henry the Fowler, 919-936.—In Henry the Fowler, Germany had for the first time a really national sovereign. Whether or no his descent from Witikind and the old independent kings of the Saxons be allowed, it cannot but be admitted that he vindicated his claim to such a descent so far as it could be vindicated by patriotism, valour, and prudence. By his marriage with Matilda, daughter of Count Dietrich of Ringelheim, he acquired for his children an undoubted claim on the affections of Saxons. Whatever he was, she at least was sprung from Witikind; but he was himself Saxon enough to represent all the interests of his people. He was born in 876, and on his father's death became Duke in 912. After having with difficulty succeeded in recovering the position which his father had held from the unwilling Conrad, he was recommended by him on his deathbed as his successor in 919. The news brought to Henry by Eberhard, Duke of Franconia, and brother of Conrad, surprised him, it is said, whilst he was out hawking, whence the name by which he is known amongst later historians, Henry the Fowler, although the name may have been given him from the fact of his being represented in pictures with a hawk on his wrist, as was not unusual in ancient portraits of princes. The election, having first been arranged on Conrad's recommendation, was formally transacted at Fritzlar in Hesse, where at a great assembly of the five nations, Henry was accepted and crowned King of the Germans by Heriger, Archbishop of Mainz. He reigned for seventeen years ;— seventeen years they were of hard and good and effectual work. Hallam allows that to Henry the Fowler and Otto I., Germany was more indebted than to any sovereign since the great Charles. More than that may be admitted by way of praise. Charles had conquered and incorporated Germany ; he had partly organised it, and in Christianity had given it an element of unity. Lewis the German had kept it from falling to pieces when the rest of the empire did so ; Conrad of Franconia had recognised the individuality of the five nations, and the half imperial, half confederate character of the royal position. But from Henry the Fowler the nation derived a working unity which lasted for three generations after him, and continued to make itself felt at intervals for a much longer period. By his wise policy and the consistent pursuit and enforcement of it, he laid the foundation of a great national system. Reading of his measures for the foundation of cities seems like reading a story of colonisation ; his extension of the boundaries of the empire entitles him to the praise of a conqueror, his victories over the Hungarians to that of a deliverer.

His Policy in Germany.—His first difficulty of course was to obtain from the dukes whom Conrad had recognised the substance as well as the show of fealty. From Eberhard of Franconia he had nothing to fear. Burchard of Swabia, cowed by the manifestation of his

power, yielded as soon as he could with a good grace.
Arnulf of Bavaria, who had himself laid claim to royalty,
was besieged by Henry at Ratisbon, and compelled to
own himself vanquished as much by the wise and conciliating policy of Henry as by his power. In 921 he
submitted honourably, became Henry's man, and was
confirmed by him in his possession of Bavaria, while
his daughter was married to Henry the Quarrelsome,
a younger son of Henry the Fowler, who ultimately
became Duke of Bavaria himself. Lorraine was propitiated in the same way after a long series of quarrels
with Charles the Simple; Giselbert the duke, who had
taken upon himself to act as an independent sovereign,
fell about 924 into the hands of Henry, who restored him
to his duchy and gave him his daughter Gerberga in
marriage. The great dukes lived quietly during the rest
of Henry's reign; from this time the duchy of Lorraine
remains a part of the German kingdom. Two petty
quarrels with Boso, King of Provence, and Rudolf, King
of Burgundy, were speedily settled; in 933 the two
kingdoms were consolidated under Rudolf under the
title of the kingdom of Arles; and henceforth, until the
extinction of the royal race, they remained faithful allies
to the German king. Such is nearly all the internal
history of Germany under Henry the Fowler, the results
of his pacificatory policy lasting unimpaired throughout
his life, and the great dukes owning themselves his
vassals and acting as faithful ones.

The Defence of the Empire against the Hungarians.—
The terrible scourge of Hungarian invasion, however,
still threatened, and did indeed more, much more, than
threaten. In 923 the Hungarians invaded Saxony in
great force, and laid it waste with such cruelty as to
amount almost to the extermination of the inhabitants,

F

Henry having no force to oppose to them, fled before them and shut himself up in Westphalia; a fortunate accident placed, however, one of their princes in his power, and in 924, on condition of his release, the barbarians consented to a peace for Saxony which was to last for nine years, and to involve the cessation of the payment of tribute. They then turned their arms in another direction, desolated Italy, and put Constantinople to ransom. The truce lasted out its time, and, as the termination approached, Henry, who had spent the intervening years in the discipline of his people, took every means of rousing in them a spirit of resistance. In the year 933 the Hungarian ambassadors appeared with their ordinary demand for tribute. Henry offered them a little dog with cropped ears and tail. He had not thrown down the challenge before he was able to prosecute the quarrel. The barbarians, indignant at the presumption of their foe, directed the whole of their forces upon his own especial dominion, Saxony and Thuringia. But the people were prepared for them; in a series of skirmishes they considerably weakened the staff of leaders, who had advanced to Westphalia; the hosts began to straggle and fell victim to the guerilla tactics of the Saxons. The main body, which had not advanced with the rest, but had stayed behind besieging Merseburg in Thuringia, fled in panic fear on the news of the destruction of their brethren, and Henry, without much loss, obtained a brilliant victory. The tribute to the barbarians, as disgraceful as it was oppressive, ceased from that time.

Henry's Administration—His Policy to the Great Dukes. —The intervening years of the truce, 924-933, and the three remaining years of the reign, were the time that Henry had to devote to developing the internal arrange-

ments by which he hoped to give unity and consistency
to his states. These measures divided themselves into
those of territorial and social regulation. The great
dukes had accepted him as their king ; most of them
survived him, and he had no wish or purpose of interfering very much with their internal governments. In
some respects he seems even to have increased their
prerogatives, as for instance in giving to Duke Arnulf
in Bavaria the right of nominating to bishoprics. Generally speaking, however, his personal influence, once
vindicated, was a sufficient motive with them ; quarrels
were averted by policy, and the kingdom assumed the
terms of a family confederacy. It is in Saxony therefore, and in those detached territories which formed the
demesne of the German crown, that the most distinct
traces of his administrative policy can be found.

The Creation and Encouragement of Towns.—The first
point to notice is the creation of towns and the encouragement of settlers. This is commonly reckoned
as the only or the great feature of Henry's reign. It
was certainly the most long-lived fruit of it. For no
one who has any knowledge of the later history of
Germany, and of the part played in it by the towns,
who recollects anything of the Hanseatic League in the
North, the commercial enterprise of such places as
Augsburg and Nüremberg, and the municipal independence fostered by the commercial adventure and the
acquisition of wealth, or how that municipal independence affected the progress of the Reformation and
whatever else on the direction of freedom and organisation that has followed the Reformation, can hesitate
to ascribe to Henry the actual origination of what
becomes a leading mark in German history. The
creation of towns by Henry the Fowler was not like

that by Edward I. in Aquitaine, where the English, although welcome perhaps, were really foreigners and protectors against a home tyranny; it is simply the binding together the scattered village populations and giving them centres of defence, of jurisdiction, and of all civilising appliances. Of the cities which Henry the Fowler built in Saxony, Meissen, Quedlinburg, Merseburg, and Goslar were the chief. In these he placed a soldierly order of burghers from whom the civic aristocracy of the Middle Ages were descended. It is stated that the assemblies of bishops and counts, and other national councils, were held by him within the cities, not as in former times on the wide plains or under the shade of the forest.

The Germans and French as Warriors.—The institution of tournaments has been attributed to Henry, but this is doubtless a mistake based on the measures which he took for teaching his people the use of arms, a teaching the efficacy of which their successes against the Hungarians sufficiently prove, and which serves to distinguish his subjects very favourably from their neighbours on the other side of the Rhine; for, strange as it may now seem, the French, from the time of Charles the Bald to the time of Philip Augustus, fell from the fame of their fathers as warriors, into great contempt. The wars of the Crusades were fought rather by Belgian and Lotharingian warriors than by Frenchmen, although the name of Franks was borne in common by their leaders. But it was an interesting topic of conversation in the reign of our English Henry II. how this apparent decadence of French valour could have been caused; and it was, by Ranulf Glanvill, set down to the account of the massacres by the Norman invaders under which the youth and spirit of Neustria fell. A succession of wise sovereigns would have attempted to recover and practice the art of war in self-defence; but the strength of France was almost immediately broken up, and, although the men of Champagne retained the character of warriors more than the rest of the French, the Normans did the bulk of the fighting, and in them only was much soldierly skill to be found. Henry the Fowler managed matters better in Germany, where the Hungarians had not shown, as did the Normans, any signs of amalgamating with the nations they devastated. And throughout the Middle Ages Germany and Lotharingia were a nursery of soldiers who, very often in the character of barbarians and Dutch reiters or routtiers, were a curse to the nations that hired them.

The Marks.—Although Henry the Fowler did not interfere much with the territories of the great dukes, he had sufficiently extensive frontiers of his own, as well as of the kingdom in general, to make the task of organisation and defence a constant occupation. He is to be remembered further as the originator and definer of the German marks, or border jurisdictions out of which, more directly than out of the great duchies, the later German states have sprung. For Prussia is but the outgrowth of the ancient march between Saxony and the Slavs; Austria is the march between the Bavarians and the Hungarians; the Saxon kingdom of to-day is the old march of Meissen; the kingdom of Sardinia is the old march of Italy. Throughout the tendency of the great duchies is to disruption; and of the marks to agglomeration. The first were wide, thinly organised, and unwieldy; the latter were each of them a nucleus of defence and civilisation round which new conquests gradually and

closely grouped themselves. The marks, or Margraviates, or marches, instituted by Henry the Fowler were
(1) Schleswig, which, having revindicated the Eyder as
the boundary of Germany, he founded as a Saxon
military colony against the invasions of the Danes,
and forced their king, Gorm the Old, to pay tribute;
(2) the march of Meissen against the Moravians,
and (3) that of Austria against the Hungarians. The
origin of the march of Brandenburg is less certainly
to be attributed to Henry; but that of Salzwedel, the
march against the Wends, which afterwards grew into
Brandenburg, probably may owe its origin to him.
Antwerp was the head of the march against the French,
and Lausitz, which lasted only a short time, being
swallowed up in the others, was also formed against
the Wends. The three first mentioned are to be
most certainly attributed to Henry, and the remaining
three with much probability. Austria he bestowed on
Leopold of Babenberg or Bamberg, the representative
of that ancient house from which sprang Duke Henry,
the defender of Paris against the Normans, and Adalbert, the rival of Conrad of Franconia in that duchy.
From Leopold sprang the first or Babenberg line of
Margraves or Dukes of Austria which became extinct
in the person of Frederick the Warrior in 1246—a
long hereditary succession of brave men. From the
Margraves of Meissen sprang the later Dukes of Saxony.
The marks of Sleswig, Salzwedel, and Lausitz did not
continue long, nor make much place in history under
those names. But north of the march of Brandenburg,
towards the region where Charles had fought his
Linonian war, Henry was obliged to content himself
with warring without organising; and further south
the Bohemians were not yet amenable to his authority.

There was in these regions a constant border warfare in which the now civilising power of the German arms made slow progress. Tributary, however, both Bohemia under its several princes, and the Obotrites under their king Miecislas, certainly became. Miecislas, moreover, embraced Christianity; Bohemia was, however, only half converted, alternating between policies of proselytism and persecution which ended in favour of Christianity in the next reign.

Henry the Fowler a Great King—His Death, 936.— Such is in brief the outline of the career and influence of this great king, of whom, if more was known, as favourable an idea might be formed as of Charles the Great or even as of the English Alfred. In him, just as in Alfred, is summed up the national hero, conqueror, colonist, deliverer; but it cannot be denied that the range of his immediate power was small compared with that which much weaker sovereigns before him had enjoyed. Like Alfred he had to be content to see himself labouring with effect only in his paternal dominions, Bavaria and Swabia being little more amenable to his rule than Northumbria and East Anglia were to Alfred. Nor, like Alfred, does he take to himself any great title. He is no more than King of the Germans, sometimes King of the Eastern Franks, sometimes even advocate of the Romans : the empire was not even offered to him, although it had been hawked about among the little kings of Burgundy and the turbulent barons of Lombardy. He never approached Italy ; but towards the end of his life, after the defeat of the Hungarians and pacification of the north, the desire of the empire is said to have come upon him, and he was prevented only by paralysis from asserting the right of the German king to the crown of Charles. As he knew his death approaching, following the example of his predecessor he called together his council of princes at Erfurt, and recommended them to elect his son Otto, whom he himself designated king. This done he retired to the monastery of Memleben, where he died a few days after, July 3, 936.

Otto I., 936–973.—The proceedings which attended the succession of Otto are very much like a repetition of those by which the election of Henry the Fowler himself was carried out. The assembly of the princes agreed to elect him, as his father had recommended ; but this time the assembly was held at Aix-la-Chapelle, instead of at Fritzlar, and immediately after the election, which was transacted by the four nations, the Franks, Saxons, Bavarians, and Swabians, the king was crowned by the Archbishop of Mainz. It is said that on this occasion for the first time the dukes executed their honorary offices in attendance on the king—the Duke of Bavaria as master of the horse, the Duke of Franconia as steward, Hermann, the Duke of Swabia, as cupbearer, and the Duke of Lorraine as purveyor-chamberlain. The Saxon duchy was vested of course in Otto himself ; but the offices as discharged on this occasion do not answer to the later ones assigned to the several electors by Charles IV. Of the circumstances of the election itself there is little record ; but it is said that a claim to the succession was put in by Henry, the eldest son born to Henry the Fowler after his accession, which, if really asserted, would be paralleled by the case of Henry I. of England, whose character as *porphyrogenitus* is so much enlarged on by Sir Francis Palgrave. A claim of less importance was also made by Thankmar, the half brother of Otto, to the estates of his mother ; both these were set aside.

Otto followed the example of his father in retaining the duchy of Saxony after his accession, instead of devolving it on a brother, as Conrad had done with Franconia; but this, as we shall see, was afterwards changed. The opening difficulties of Otto's reign were also like those of his father's; the desire of independence on the part of the great dukes gave rise to both; and the struggle is carried on in detail through the several duchies.

The Character of the Reign.—The whole reign of Otto is, however, a series of wars, several going on at the same time, and in so far it resembles that of Charles the Great. Without ascribing to Otto the full glory of Charles, a very high place among his followers cannot be refused him. As far as regards Germany, the difficulties of Otto were greater, and his means were smaller; and although in universal history Charles has left a broader and deeper mark, it may be questioned whether Otto did not secure more firmly than Charles did the actual purposes for which he worked, or left a more consolidated power to his successors. To attempt an exact chronological resumé of the earlier years of Otto would be simply to give a string of dates, names, and battles. It will be less puzzling to arrange under the heads of the duchies the principal changes and struggles and their causes.

The First Civil War, 938–941.—Strange to say, the first difficulties arose in Saxony, owing to the jealousies of the nobles, who, being vassals of the king as Duke of Saxony, declined to show feudal respect to the Duke of Franconia, of whom they held other fiefs. These disputes of course concerned Thuringia and Hesse, the debatable country between Saxony and Franconia, which had been sometimes attached to the one and sometimes to the other. Eberhard, Duke of Franconia,

smarting under the insults of the Saxons, burned a
town on the Weser, and provoked Otto to punish
him. Eberhard was fined 100 talents in horses, the
inferior nobles were condemned to the disgrace of the
"Hunescar," to carry a dog on their shoulders for a
space of two leagues. This disgrace sank deep into
the mind of Eberhard, who took part in every rebellion
against Otto until his death in 939. Thankmar, the
son of Henry by his first divorced wife, was the next
transgressor ; and his rebellion has more political
meaning. Otto, it is related, whilst retaining the
duchy of Saxony in his own hands, administered it by
the service of a Count Siffrid ; this Count died, and
Thankmar, who was a cousin of his, not unnaturally
looked for the succession to the county. Otto, however, who had refused him his mother's estates, was
not likely to put him into so important a place, and
entrusted it to Count Gero. Thankmar took up arms
in conjunction with Eberhard, who at the first was so
successful as to take prisoner Henry the Quarrelsome,
brother of King Otto. But the triumph was short.
Otto advanced against Eresburg, which was in Thankmar's hands, and was gladly received by the citizens.
The rebel brother was killed in a church, and Eberhard
releasing his prisoner (having persuaded him into
rebellion), was pardoned and the war ended.

Conspiracy of Henry the Quarreller, 939.—But the
very next year, 939, the other brother, Henry the
Quarreller, originated a new conspiracy in which he
drew not only Eberhard but Giselbert of Lorraine,
the king's brother-in-law and his own. It is difficult
to penetrate the object of this conspiracy, the immediate aim of which was to dethrone Otto. Henry was
doubtless tempted by the idea of being in his brother's

place, but Giselbert and Eberhard had each a selfish design in view ; Giselbert wished, it appears, to restore the kingdom of Lotharingia in his own person as he had done in the reign of Henry the Fowler. Eberhard, rather to place himself on the throne of Germany. But the war which they provoked, although eventful, was short. Otto's forces summarily defeated Henry and Giselbert near Cologne. Henry, after being besieged for two months in Merseburg, surrendered and was allowed to retire from Saxony into Lorraine. In Lorraine, Otto was by no means so successful as his cause deserved : his failure encouraged Eberhard to join openly in the war, and Lewis of France now joined the league. But the luck suddenly changed. Otto's general, Conrad the Wise, and Udo, brother of Herman, Duke of Swabia, met Eberhard and Giselbert at Andernach. Eberhard was slain in battle, Giselbert drowned in the Rhine ; in one moment Otto was freed from his most dangerous enemies and stood secure. The French king fled out of Alsace ; and Conrad, King of Burgundy, commended himself and his kingdom as vassal to Otto.

The attempted Reorganisation of the Duchies.—Otto was now in a position nearly as good as his father's had been. This year 939 saw him with two duchies at his disposal, Franconia vacated by Eberhard, and Lorraine by Giselbert. But Bavaria also was lawfully vacant ; Arnulf died in 937, and Otto had not yet received the homage of his successor. Lorraine, the king gave to his quarrelsome brother Henry, Franconia to Conrad the Wise (or Red), Count of Naven, Worms, and Speyer, the ancestor of the Franconian emperors and son-in-law of Otto.[1] But Henry the Quarrelsome

[1] He married Luitgarde, daughter of Otto.

did not keep Lorraine for more than a year; his old propensities made him intolerable; and Otto, after trying some intermediate experiments, gave the duchy to Conrad to hold with Franconia, which he did for several years. In 953 Otto gave it to his brother Bruno, Archbishop of Cologne, who divided it into Upper and Lower Lorraine and administered it by two dukes, himself bearing the title of Archduke. There are many anomalies in this arrangement of Lorraine which would be hard to explain: in particular, the lower nobility, as they should be called, did not hold feudally of the duke but of the empire, the duke only being feudal lord over the vassals of his own demesne. Amongst these tenants *in capite* as they at this time became, were the three Bishops of Toul, Metz, and Verdun, whose territory was so long afterwards the bone of contention between Charles V. and Francis I., and the loss of which broke the proud and tenacious spirit of the former sovereign. Henry the Quarrel-some being ousted from Lorraine was planted in Bavaria (he had married a daughter of Duke Arnulf), and there founded a family which continued the Saxon line in the person of Henry II. The old Dukes of Bavaria descended from Ludolf and Arnulf, subsided into the Counts of Scheyren, from whom the present house of Bavaria, the Wittelsbachers, is said to descend. Otto thus, instead of reconciling enmities by the gift of his daughters as Henry the Fowler had done, re-placed his enemies in their duchies by his own firm friends. Herman of Swabia gave his only child in marriage to the king's son, and Germany was again a family party. Unfortunately family parties, even when exemplified on this august scale, are not always peaceful ones, and as the result shows, this of Otto's furnishes one more to a very common stock of historical parallels. Otto had married during his father's lifetime Eadgitha, daughter of Edward the elder, King of England, sister of Athelstan and granddaughter of Alfred. She brought him a son named Ludolf, who was born in 934, before Otto's accession, and a daughter Luitgarde, married to Conrad the Wise (or Red): she died in 947. Almost immediately after her death, Otto declared Ludolf king, his partner and successor, and provided for him for the present by the gift of Swabia, 950, marrying him to the daughter of Duke Herman. For a time this worked well ; but when, in 951, Otto married again, and it was reported that the children of the new wife would have a share in the kingdom although no son was yet born (until 955), Ludolf, just as the sons of Lewis the Pious had done, took alarm and prepared to rebel.

Second Civil War, 953.—Otto had now become King of Italy, and this seems to have shaken the faith or the affection of the Germans ; he had much less standing ground in Saxony than Henry the Fowler had had, and Saxony, jealous as of old, upheld Ludolf. Hermann Billung, the royal deputy or duke under Otto in Saxony, was faithful, but the nobles widely rebelled, and unhappily Conrad the Wise, the brother-in-law of Ludolf, joined the conspiracy. Again North Germany is banded against South, for only Henry of Bavaria continued faithful to his brother. Even the Archbishop of Mainz was a rebel. Otto was prompt in his measures, and, almost as soon as hostilities were begun, hurried to Mainz, surprised Ludolf, and compelled him to reveal the names of his allies. In a council at Fritzlar they were condemned to exile. But Ludolf, although he escaped for the time, did not become obedient : again he took up arms, and again was compelled to ask pardon. Now he was besieged in Mainz, now he was victorious in Bavaria. In 953 all Germany was in arms. The Hungarians were summoned by Conrad and Ludolf to aid them against Otto. Bruno, the Archbishop of Cologne, was ready to crown Conrad king. Whether it was really the discontent of Germany provoked by the Italian measures of Otto, or the jealousy of the old friends and companions of his difficulties, or the outbreak of more concealed causes finding an opportunity by these jealousies, it is impossible to say. For five years more or less the storm lasted. At length Bruno and Conrad, with the Archbishop, returned to their allegiance, and Ludolf, although never quite reconciled with his father, was reduced to insignificance. He died in 957. Conrad had to resign Lorraine, which was entrusted to Bruno, and died soon after, leaving Franconia to his son. Swabia was taken from Ludolf and given to Burchard II., who married Duke Henry of Bavaria's daughter. And very shortly after Otto disengaged himself from the ancient connection of his house with the Saxons, by making Hermann Billung, the allodial lord of Lüneberg, the head of the most venerable house in Saxony, who had already acted for some years as duke under him, full Duke of Saxony. He retained for his family only the hereditary allods of his ancestors.

Otto's Imperial Position.—In all this previous history it is easy to see that Otto was rising out of the position with which his father had been content, and gradually becoming more of an emperor. Germany was not to him, as it had been to Henry, all in all ; still less was Saxony the object of his peculiar care and the source of his strength. Into the designs of Otto in Italy, and his restoration of reality to the empire, an account will be given in the next chapter. And with the beginning of Otto's imperial projects we lose much of the clearness with which we have been able hitherto to analyse German history.

Defeat of the Hungarians on the Lechfeld, 955.—It seems strange to find, whilst all this dynastic striving and conspiring is on foot, that the Hungarians are still annually ravaging Germany. Yet so it is; every year they devastated the country as far as the Rhine. In 955, however, at the invitation of the unhappy Ludolf, and seeing the difficulties in which Otto was involved, they marched into Germany with a larger force than they had ever had before. Luckily Otto was ready for them. He overtook them at Augsburg, which they were besieging, and on the Lechfeld, on August 10, inflicted on them such a defeat that they never dared to enter Germany again. This may well be called one of the decisive battles of the world.

Wars with the Bohemians and the Danes, 937–950.— The frontier wars which had employed Henry the Fowler were also a constant work for Otto. With Bohemia, relapsed into heathenism, he waged war for thirteen years, from 937 to 950. The last year saw the complete subjugation of Boleslas, and the conversion of the nation followed. In 948 the Danes challenged Otto to war; he invaded and overran the country and compelled Harold the king to hold his kingdom as his vassal. He insisted also on his being baptized, with his wife and child Swein, to whom the conqueror gave his own name and called him Swend Otto. By way of completing the matter, the country was divided into three dioceses, which were made suffragan to the Archbishop of Hamburg. The King

Harold is Harold Bluetooth, and Swend Otto is no other than Sweyn the conqueror of our king, Ethelred the Unready, and father of Canute, King of England.

Extension of Otto's Empire.—The Slav border was strengthened by continual extension. The empire was extended to the Oder, and the whole of that side of the country placed under the Margrave of Lausitz; for the Christianised population, an archbishop see was erected at Magdeburg, to which Brandenburg and Havelberg were made suffragan, with the addition of new sees at Meissen, Merseberg [Zeitz], and Naumburg. Further north, among the Obotrites and to the east of them, he founded the church of Oldenburg, afterwards Lübeck, under the archbishopric of Hamburg. The rest of the history of Otto, the first and greatest, belongs to Italy, and to a region of study which will be treated in the following chapter. The aim of the present chapter is to give an adequate idea of the Germany which Otto governed, and of the condition of his kingdom at the time that he united it with the heavy and soulless companionship of the empire. The ground, although not abounding in romantic incident or much play of character, has a clear matter of fact aspect, that, whilst it presents us with no great problems, repays study by fixing itself in the memory and preparing the mind to understand intelligently the complications and developments of the coming time. Germany is now feudalised, Christianised, organised under its dukes and margraves and bishops. Its weakness in the still subsisting national divisions which have but to a small degree closed in is apparent. But at its head is a monarch who, after many struggles, has made himself the master of the whole; no longer content like his father with the actual sovereignty of the strongest nation, but able to balance his throne on the equal obedience of all. His German kingdom is something like an empire now. But the imperial title is still to be won, and the imperial dignity carries everywhere with it new dangers and new manners of death.

IMPORTANT DATES

Henry I. (the Fowler), 918.
Truce with the Hungarians, 924.
Renewal of war with the Hungarians, 933.
Henry's death, 936.
Otto the Great succeeds, 936.
The First Civil War, 938–941.
Defeat of the Hungarians near Augsburg, 955.

CHAPTER VI

Europe in the middle of the tenth century—The political condition
of Italy—Otto I. and the Papacy—Death of Otto, 973—His
character and work—The fatal connection of Germany and
Italy—Otto II., 973–983—His character—Otto III., 983–1000—
The year 1000.

*Condition of the Continent in the Middle of the Tenth
Century.* — Early history busies itself so much with
the movements of kings and princes, and depends so
entirely on the evidence of those who watched, like
the biographers of the saints, chiefly the personal inci-
dents of the periods they were employed upon, that
it is difficult to follow the series of events where the
chief actor is not present. From the year 962 to the
year 973, Otto the Great was constantly employed in
Italy; nay, from 951 to 973, from his first visit to
Lombardy, his thoughts and acts were so taken
up with Italian and imperial politics that, in the
personal string of his history, Germany is almost
lost sight of. It cannot be said, or even supposed,
that the intervening years were a time of peace for
Germany ; still, the national or tribal jealousies subsisted, and were only temporarily and intermittently
smothered by the strength, or by the family policy
of the king. Still on the north and east of Germany
were pressing on warlike hosts of barbarians, alien in
race, language, and religion ; or only so far humanised,
Germanised, and Christianised as to render them more
dangerous, because more secret, subtle, and experienced

enemies. Still on the French frontier Lorraine was
a disputed territory between the perishing Karolings
and the Germans, although by repeated conquest, and
repeated commendations, it had become, so far as the
law of nations could make it, a part of Germany. But
that the Kings of France were now so weak, and their
great vassals content with the substance of power,
this borderland would have been a scene of perpetual
war. Nor indeed was the war that desolated less than
continual, for on every opportunity the claims of the
French and German titles were asserted by the chief
of the nobles, and constantly the one or the other
power was being dragged in. After the death of the
unhappy Ludolf in 957, and the administration of the
Archduke Bruno from 959 downwards, little is heard
of the events of Lotharingian history during the rest
of the reign. In 955, Duke Henry the Quarrelsome of
Bavaria died; and although he left his dukedom to a
son of the same name, and not less quarrelsome than
his father, the son continued steady in his allegiance
so long as his uncle reigned. So also in Franconia,
which from 955, the year of Duke Conrad's death, was
administered, during the minority of his successor, by
the Archbishop of Mainz, William, the son of Otto.
Swabia had continued in the hands of Burchard, who
died the same year with his master.

Germany in the Middle of the Tenth Century.—The
intention of this book is primarily to describe German
history, and to diverge as little as possible into French
and Italian history. The interest of the remaining
years of the Saxon dynasty is, however, so completely
Italian that it is impossible now to avoid giving a
glance across the Alps. The year 950 has now been
reached. Italy has been left to itself for nearly fifty

years; in fact, since the time of the Emperor Arnulf, no German king has set foot there. A happy time for Germany comparatively, for during it, in spite of many civil and border wars, the process of consolidation and civilisation has been going on rapidly; the influence of Christianity increasing; learning and all the arts of peace enjoying an occasional breathing time; and the idea of national unity obtaining some sort of recognition. King Otto, from his favourite city of Magdeburg, or on frequent expeditions through his demesnes, or in constant border warfare, is showing himself necessary to Germany, and by his foundation of cities, churches, and sees, by his arrangements of duchies and marks, by his renewal of the missions of royal judges, and by his bestowal of regalia on the prelates, is preparing for the imperial arrangement of Germany. In spite of rebellions, quarrels, difficulties, wars of every kind, Germany is growing stronger and stronger; France is being torn to pieces; Italy is losing any little semblance of unity and strength that it had gathered under the administration of the Karolings.

The Condition of Italy.—In fact, looking at Italy now, all that can be asked is what had the Frank empire, the Frank.dominion done for it? Charles the Great had found it desolated under Lombard tyranny, and claimed by various titles, none of which were the owners strong enough to vindicate. The Lombard kings in the north and the Lombard dukes in the south, the Exarchate of Ravenna and the district of Calabria, the last relics of the Byzantine dominion, the papal claims and those of the Roman nobles and people in central Italy—all these are historical factors difficult to define and impossible to feel interest in. By the middle of the tenth century (nearly two cen-

turies after the delivery of the Papacy and the donation
of Pipin), *i.e.* after a century of separate government
away from the rest of the Karoling inheritances, there
are to be still found factors difficult to define and unable to inspire interest.   The names of the petty rulers
have ceased to be Lombard and become German ;
there are Adalberts and Lamberts and Berengars and
Bernards, instead of Grimwalds and Landulfs.   But the
wretched medley is little altered ; the old adhesive
Greek jurisdiction still holds out in the South, but the
Papacy and the empire are hopelessly degraded : he
who would pick the imperial crown out of the mire
must stoop rather than climb, and instead of coming
as the defender must appear as the judge, the arbiter,
the giver, the avenger of the Papacy.   Since the deposition of Charles the Fat no Karoling had been
King of Italy.   Charles the Simple and his descendants
confined their pretensions to France and Lorraine, retaining a portion of the former by the consent of their
great vassals, and obtaining a portion of the latter as
vassals of the German kings.   In default of the hereditary line the Popes had played two sets of emperors off
against each other ; and while Kings of Italy had been
chosen sometimes with and sometimes without the
imperial name, emperors had been crowned sometimes
with and sometimes without the Italian dominion.
The Italian kingdom at the widest meant only Lombardy and Tuscany ; it frequently meant nothing at
all.   For this shadow there had competed first Berengar
of Friuli, who, on his mother's side, was descended from
Charles the Great, first with Guy of Spoleto, then with
Lambert his son, and last with King Lewis of Arles,
the son of Boso, also descended remotely from the
Karolings.   From 888–924 Berengar maintained the

rivalry. Under the name of Kings of Italy, during the following period, is to be found Rudolf of Burgundy, 922–926, Hugh of Arles, 926–945, and Lothair, his son, 945–950. This Lothair was the husband of Adelheid, who brought Otto the Great into Italy. Berengar II., son of the Marquis Adalbert of Tuscany, and a daughter of the first Berengar, in the hope of acquiring Italy, poisoned Lothair and imprisoned Adelheid, who, as daughter of King Rudolf, had some sort of title to Italy herself. From her imprisonment Adelheid, by the assistance of her chaplain, escaped to Canossa, to the protection of the Marquis Azzo, and by his advice sent to ask the aid of Otto. This was in 951. Otto had been a widower for four years. He had just completed the war against the Bohemians, and had not yet been disturbed by the ambition of Ludolf; he readily accepted the invitation, drove Berengar from Pavia, and married Queen Adelheid. He was himself elected King of Italy; but, being coldly received by the Pope, returned to Germany without the imperial title, leaving Pavia and Lombardy, which had yielded without a blow, under the charge of Conrad the Wise. The next year, however, Berengar submitted, came to Otto at Magdeburg, and became Otto's vassal for the kingdom of Italy. Observe Otto, as yet only King of Germany, gives or accepts the commendation of the kingdom of Italy as a fief. The war with Ludolf occupied Otto for several years from this time, and he had no leisure for Italy, where Berengar had almost immediately cast off the yoke and begun to play the tyrant, until in 956 when he sent Ludolf, after his submission, to represent him there; but Ludolf died on the expedition, although not before he had conquered the kingdom of Berengar.

Otto and the Papacy, 962–973.—It was the condition of

the Papacy which brought Otto the second time to Italy. The abuses of the Roman see in the tenth century justified and demanded external interference. When John XII. invited Otto to deliver him from Berengar and Adalbert, received him and crowned him emperor on the 2nd of February 962, a step of vast importance to Europe had been taken. As soon as Otto had left Rome, John turned round, and began to intrigue with Adalbert; Otto returned, the Pope and Adalbert fled before him, while the Romans received him as a deliverer, and in a solemn agreement with him promised never to make another Pope without the consent of the emperor. He then deposed John and made Leo VIII. Pope in his place. But as soon as he had departed John returned, and on his death in 964 a new Pope, Benedict V., was chosen and Leo again rejected. Again Otto came to the rescue, but this time he was obliged to besiege Rome, and on its surrender carried off Benedict to Germany. Leo, whom he re-established, died the next year. The great officers of Rome then visited Otto in Saxony to obtain his leave for an election, and on their return, by Otto's permission, John XIII. was chosen. The same year Burchard, Duke of Swabia, defeated Adalbert in Italy and made Otto irresistible. John XIII. was not a wise Pope; relying on the imperial support, he offended and persecuted the nobles; they expelled him from Rome and imprisoned him. Again Otto is brought from Germany in 967, delivers the Pope, and this time hangs the rebels, and has his son Otto, who in 961 had been crowned King of Germany, now crowned emperor. After remaining for a long time in Italy, and settling the affairs of the German Church, holding councils, negotiating for the marriage of his son Otto with Theophanô, the daughter of the Byzantine emperor, Romanus II., with whom Apulia and Calabria were to be given up to him ; then conducting war with the Greeks, and finally succeeding in getting the lady into his hands and imposing tribute on the Calabrian and Apulian Greeks.

Death and Description of Otto the Great, 973.—This done, he returned to his dear Magdeburg, and spent his last days, as his father had spent his, in the neighbourhood of Merseburg, and at Memleben, where his father had died. He also died, on the 7th of May 973, and was buried next his English wife Edith, in the Cathedral at Magdeburg. A fair picture of Otto is drawn by his own contemporaries; and it is that of a true venerable German hero, full of life and strength. A man of great height and muscular strength ; scanty grey hair, but a magnificent long beard reaching to his waist, unlike the Karolings, who wore short beards or none at all. A broad, shaggy chest ; a spare athletic figure ; gait rapid and yet dignified ; his dress always the old Saxon habit of his father and grandfather. Most pious, most constant; severe but gentle where he could be gentle; cheerful and liberal ; a most faithful friend. More fortunate than Charles the Great, he was able to learn both reading and writing (not from his English wife, for it was after her death that he began his studies), and he could speak the language both of his German and of his Slav subjects. There had been no such king, say the historians, since Charles the Great. He died in a good old age, and left all his kingdoms in peace.

The Value of His Work.—It might be asked, what did he gain by his acquisition of the empire ? What good did he do to himself, or to Germany, or to the Papacy, or to Italy ? It would be hard to answer the question with anything like satisfaction. To Germany he brought

from the very first step he took for the deliverance of
Adelheid, nothing but sorrow, the renewing of half
slumbering jealousies, the opening of half-healed wounds.
He broke up the peace of the family amongst which
the real as well as the nominal jurisdiction of Germany
was divided; impaired the hold which his personal
greatness had upon it; and set in arms against himself
his own son, his brothers, and the most faithful of his
servants and friends. It is true that all these things
were, so far as his personal influence went, remedied
before his death; he died supreme, and was buried in
the midst of his people. But at how great a cost,—
the loss of his dearest child and of the confidence of
his best friends! Still he survived those old friends
and found new ones who were faithful.

The Fatal Connection of Germany with Italy.—For
Germany, however, the fatal alliance with Italy was
the beginning of unnumbered woes, and hardly less so
for Italy herself.[1] Still Otto cannot be blamed for the
evils that followed from his great success. As for the
counterbalancing gains, it is difficult to see what they
were beyond the semi-divine title of Cæsar and Augustus.
Italy was a constant drain of blood and treasure upon
Germany from the year 962 to the year 1866; nine
hundred years of wasted men and money. It is true
that sometimes great good resulted to Italy from German
interference; but never anything but harm resulted to
Germany from the Italian dominion. There was lost
the honour of Otto II., and there the life of Otto III.
was wasted; there was wrought the humiliation of
Henry IV., the one great failure of Frederick Barbarossa,
the profound, astounding ruin of Frederick II., "the
wonder of the world"; and there the new empire that

[1] See in a later chapter.

Charles V. had founded, shaken from its very foundation by Italian enmities, lost its strength and credit, and parted with the very name of empire under the defeats inflicted by Napoleon Bonaparte. Was there in Germany itself a basis or groundwork of unity which might have supported a great self-contained, unenlarged empire? But it is no question that so long as the dead carcase of Italy was attached to the living body of Germany there could be no healthy action for Germany. And, to avoid metaphor, it may be said that never since the time of Charles the Great, and of course never before, had there been sufficient union and consistency in the mass of the kindred nations of Germany to make it safe for a moment to withdraw the ordering governing hand, or to distract the ruling head with foreign cares. The annexation of Italy meant the disruption of Germany; but the fact that Germany could be so easily and so generally broken up, shows that the annexation of Italy was not the cause, but the occasion of disruption; that the crack and flaw was in the mass itself, and the pains that might have been well spent on the welding of it, being diverted to other purposes, would have left the cracks and flaws to spread, even if the troubles of the Italian connection had not been so great as to shake it, thus cracked and flawed, to pieces.

Otto II., 973–983.—The first result of the Italian connection was the emperor Otto II., son of Otto and Adelheid, a very degenerate son of so great a father. He was born in 955, elected King of Germany at Worms in 961, crowned at Aix-la-Chapelle, and crowned emperor at Rome in 967. But although he had borne these dignities for several years and had published edicts as king and emperor, his title to the entire succession was not considered complete until he had received the oaths of fealty from his vassals. No one yet thought of refusing them, however, and he was un- animously recognised as king and emperor in his father's stead. As he was only eighteen years old, the Empress Adelheid undertook to act as prime minister. Otto, however, was not inclined to submit to much interference, and very soon drove his mother into exile at the court of her brother, Conrad of Burgundy. She was, some time after, recalled, but finally left her son and settled down at her old home at Pavia, where she made herself useful in managing the Italian vassals. She must have been a woman of considerable power, as, independently of the influence which she exerted over her husband, she seems to have kept the German court in order whilst she was present in it. Anyhow, as soon as she had left, the troubles of Otto II. began, first with Bavaria and afterwards with France and Lorraine. These troubles with a constant Slav war on the north-eastern frontier comprise nearly all the German history of the reign of Otto II. ; and the circumstances are so much like those of the similar quarrels in the two preceding reigns, that it will be unnecessary to dwell upon them at any length. Bavaria was the only one of the interior duchies that gave him any trouble. Saxony was faithful all his time under Benno or Bernard Billung, who was put in his father's place the year of Otto's accession. Otto of Franconia was faithful all his time. Alemannia or Swabia was given in 973 to Otto, son of Ludolf, nephew of the emperor, and he also was faithful all his time.

Bavarian War, 973-978.—The Bavarian race was, however, incurably quarrelsome. Henry the Wrangler conspired with the Czechs of Bohemia and some of the Bavarian bishops, especially Abraham, Bishop of Freising. Otto learned the plot and summoned Henry to court ; he attended, and was detained there for some time. On his release he returned into Bavaria, and renewed his plot. Otto then marched after him, and again imprisoned him. He escaped and took refuge in Bohemia. Otto followed him, and was beaten by the Bohemians at Pilsen. Henry then threw himself into Passau, where he was besieged by the emperor and afterwards pardoned. But his duchy was partly broken up, and what remained was taken from him and given to Otto of Swabia, the son of Ludolf, who held it until his death in 982. This struggle extends over the first five years of Otto's reign, and originated undoubtedly in the wish of Henry to make Bavaria an independent kingdom, rather than in any idea of unseating Otto. Otto gained no fame or advantage from the struggle, but does not, on the other hand, seem to have conducted himself with much harshness. His administration in Germany may thus be favourably compared with his conduct in Italy.

The War in Lorraine, 978-980.—The troubles in Lorraine resulted from the uncomfortable and unsettled relations with the remaining Karolings. It seems almost incredible that the emperors, who maintained their court at Aix-la-Chapelle, should have governed Lorraine with such a weak hand, whilst they devoted all their strength to extend the empire towards the east and south. But there can be no doubt that the confusion in Lorraine was owing to the machination of the Karolings, and that the Saxon emperors did not wish by crushing the Karolings to give the Counts of Paris and Dukes of France the chance of raising a strong monarchy at Paris on the ruins of the weak

monarchy of Laon.   They constantly gave way to
Charles the Simple and Louis d'Outremer on the
subject of Lorraine, and these took advantage of the
freedom, which their own weakness gave them, to
trouble the empire.   The present struggle seems to
have been a relic of the administration of the Archduke
Bruno, and to have begun before the reign of Otto.
The county of Mons was the bone of contention at
first, being disputed by Rainer, the nephew of old Duke
Giselbert, who had been deprived of it by Bruno.
Otto does not seem to have been successful against
him.   The duchy itself Otto gave to Charles, the son
of Lewis d'Outremer, and brother of the French king
Lothair ; but Lothair himself imagined that he had
claims upon it, and undertook to revenge the cause
of the dispossessed Rainer.   He made a sudden inroad
into the empire, advanced rapidly as far as Aix-la-
Chapelle, and all but succeeded in catching Otto and
his wife at dinner.   Otto retaliated, collected his forces,
and driving Lothair I., who had enjoyed himself for
three days at Aix, before him, pursued him, ravaging
the country on his way, as far as Paris.   Whilst Otto
was returning, Lothair had his revenge, the emperor
losing part of his baggage in one river and a great
part of his army in another.   In 978 Otto again invaded France, but with no final success, until in 980
the two potentates met in a friendly way near Rheims,
and Lothair resigned his claims on Lorraine.   Immediately after that pacification, Otto was called away
into Italy.

Otto's Italian Expedition, 980.—If the annalists are to
be taken literally, and if they did not confuse the dates
of Otto's expeditions, he must have made at least three
journeys into Italy: the first immediately after his ac-

cession, the second in 980, and the third in 981. But it would seem that he really made but one, and that in the autumn of the year 980, after the conclusion of the peace with France. He had three objects in view, the humiliation of the Lombard towns and nobles who had expressed the utmost contempt for him, and were building castles in and out of the cities to strengthen themselves against him ; the protection of the Pope Benedict VII., who had done his best to support the imperial cause ; and the annexation to the empire of the Greek provinces in the South, which were partly in the hands of the Saracens, and which had been promised to Otto as the inheritance of his wife Theophanô, by the Byzantine court. In the first of these objects he was apparently successful ; he held a great diet at Roncaglia, and there did justice upon his enemies and restored peace. Thence he went to Rome, where in March 981 he held with the Pope two ecclesiastical councils. He was next employed, if not so successfully, in Apulia and Calabria, whither he now hastened. The Western writers are divided in opinion as to his object in this war, some even supposing that he claimed the Greek crown in the right of his wife, others that he was pro-voked by the refusal of the Greeks to pay any longer the tribute from these provinces due to Theophanô. Probably he wished to complete the kingdom of Italy by the conquest of Magna Græca, the fatal conquest which no German prince but Frederick II. ever really was enabled to make. He descended into Apulia : the wretched Greeks called in the Saracens against him. The Greeks,[1] having recovered this territory from the Saracens with the aid of the Emperor Lewis II., had governed it as the "Theme of Lombardy," by an officer

---

[1] Gibbon, "The Decline and Fall of the Roman Empire," c. 56.

or catapan seated at Bari, and had held out successfully by treachery against Otto the Great when he wished to enforce the claims, as he considered them, of his daughter-in-law. Finding Otto II. prepared to attack them they called in their old enemies to their help.

Otto's Death in Italy, 983.—In 982 Otto won a great victory at Cotrone, and slew such a great number of Saracens as to earn himself the title by which Otto of Freising commemorates him : "The pale death of the Saracens." A few days after they had their revenge ; they surprised Otto near the coast, where he was wandering with his nephew, Otto of Swabia, and some of the other princes, and surrounded him in great numbers. Otto on horseback swam out to a ship which was within sight and which carried him to Rossano, where he escaped by swimming from his deliverers, who were anxious to put him to ransom. He made no further attempt on Calabria, but, after seizing Benevento, returned northwards and held a diet at Verona, where he bestowed Bavaria on Henry, Duke of Carinthia, son of Berthold, son of Arnulf, and procured the election of his son Otto as his successor. This year he again visited Rome, and on the death of Benedict VII. placed John XIV. on the throne of S. Peter. One of the new Pope's first acts was to receive the last confession of Otto. He fell sick at Rome, made his will, and died on the 7th of December 983. He was buried in the vestibule or nave of S. Peter's.

The Character of Otto II.—It is impossible to say much about Otto II. Had he been more successful we should probably have heard less of his faults, but he was unlucky both in Germany and in Italy, and did not live long enough to redeem his misfortunes. He was a little red-haired, red-faced, violent, passionate man ;

according to Thietmar, who knew him, he grew more temperate and less tyrannical as he grew older ; but it is to be remembered that he was only twenty-eight when he died, and that, although the beginning of his reign had been without the usual troubles of a contested election, he had been subject to a series of mishaps, more annoying perhaps than serious, in everything that he set his hand to. He is described, moreover, as liberal and as a faithful friend ; his friends certainly were faithful to him, and that is much in his favour.

Otto III., 983–1000.—Otto II.'s wife, Theophanô, bore him one son, Otto, " Mirabilia mundi," as he was called, born in the year 980, and now therefore only three years old. There might have been a stormy succession, but it blew over with only a little risk. As soon as the news of the death of Otto II. reached Aix-la-Chapelle, the Archbishops of Ravenna and Mainz took and crowned the little heir on Christmas day. No elaborate form of election could have taken place, but none was needed ; the succession had descended hereditarily for two reigns, the son of the last emperor succeeding. There was no other son ; for the first time the great Saxon house, the great German empire, is represented by a little child. But there were agnates : there was Henry (the Quarrelsome's son) of Bavaria, who had claimed his duchy and was as anxious as ever to be made a king. He put in a claim to be guardian of the little Otto, and by the connivance of the Archbishop of Cologne succeeded in getting hold of him. With this pledge in his hands, he prevailed on a body of Saxon nobles to salute him as king at Quedlinburg at Easter 984 ; but the attempt shocked the sounder thinkers of the body, and ended in a fiasco. The faithful Bernard

Billung headed the loyal party, and with him the Archbishop of Mainz and Conrad of Alemannia, a descendant of the former race of dukes who had been put into
that duchy on the death of Otto in 983. By these men
Henry was compelled to give up the little king, and by
the following Easter harmony was restored. Then at
Quedlinburg a court was held with great solemnity at
which Duke Bernard acted as master of the horse,
Henry of Bavaria as cupbearer, Conrad as chamberlain,
and Henry the younger as steward ; the dukes of the
Obotrites, Slavs, and Bohemians likewise submitted.
The two empresses, Adelheid, wife of Otto I., and
Theophanô, wife of Otto II., acted as regents,[1] and the
child was committed for his education to Bernard,
Bishop of Hildesheim. He owed his later teaching,
after 995, to the very remarkable scholar Gerbert, who
afterwards became Pope Sylvester II.—a man of the
greatest learning and research in every accessible de-
partment of knowledge, and capable of inspiring his
pupil with the greatest ardour for knowledge and with
great affection for himself. During this long minority
the warlike reputation of Germany was sustained by
Otto, Duke of Franconia, the son of Conrad the Wise,
who played the same part with the young Otto as the
first Otto of Saxony had done with Lewis, the son of
Arnulf the emperor, and occupied his duchy without a
single act of rebellion or cause of offence for fifty-five
years. [During Otto's minority Eckhard of Meissen
drove back the Slavonic invaders and averted all danger
from the Poles and Bohemians.] The first ten or twelve
years of the reign were free from internal warfare.
Lothair of France made in 985 an ineffectual attempt to
conquer Lorraine, and the barbarians on the eastern

---

[1] Adelheid during Otto's minority ruled Italy from Pavia.

H

frontier were in continual motion ; but partly by policy and partly by force they were at length subdued, and in the year 996 Otto, now sixteen, made his first expedition into Italy, and was crowned emperor at Rome.

The Year 1000.—At this moment great issues were commencing for the empire and for the world. There were many things which made the era important. The utter collapse and ruin of the Karolings in France, the destruction of the once formidable power of England under Ethelred by the Danes, and the abject condition of the Popes might not unnaturally hold out to the mind of a young and enthusiastic prince, nurtured on the choicest and most abstruse knowledge of the time, a dream of universal dominion. In the next chapter will be found a survey of German influence on the Continent, as wielded by the hands of Otto, and also of the condition of the Papacy and of the Church under his pious successor St. Henry. Already it has been seen that in Otto the German kingdom has become clearly and decidedly hereditary and with it the imperial dignity. The next century exhibits the imperial dignity realised to its fullest extent by Henry III. and abased to its lowest depth by his unhappy son.

IMPORTANT DATES

Otto visits Italy, 951.
Coronation of Otto by Pope John XII., 962.
Embassy sent to Constantinople to ask for the hand of Theophanô for Otto's son, 968.
Marriage of Theophanô to Otto's son at Rome, 972.
Death of Otto I., 973.
Otto II., 973–983.

Civil war in Germany, 973-978.
War in Lorraine, 978-980.
Italian expedition, 980.
Otto's death, 983.
Otto III., 983-1002.
Failure of Lothair of France to conquer Lorraine, 985.
Death of Theophanô, 991.

CHAPTER VII

Otto III.—His coronation at Rome—Second and third visits to Italy —His last visit to Italy, 1000—His death, 1002—Condition of the Empire—Accession of Henry II.—His Wars with the Bohemians, Poles, and Flemish—England's connection with Lorraine and Flanders—Henry's visit to Italy—Coronation at Rome—Henry's third visit to Rome—His death and character—His relations with the German Church—Ecclesiastical organisation of Germany.

The Aspirations of Otto III.—Although it has been stated without any adequate grounds that the approach of the year 1000 A.D. was viewed by the more ignorant with alarm, as a likely date for the ending of their present dispensation, it was certainly regarded with very little feeling of awe at Rome or at Aix-la-Chapelle. The Romans went on their own way, and the youthful emperor nursed dreams of a high noble ambition which were never to be fulfilled. The beginning of the new century was to be the inauguration of a reign of universal order and justice; Rome was to be the seat of both temporal and spiritual supremacy; a German king and a German Pope would give laws from the Eternal city to the whole Church and to the whole world. Otto's early teaching had been full, no doubt, of such high lessons. Whatever he may have learned from Adelheid and Theophanó, and they could tell him much of high enterprise and sovereign magnificence, from Bernard he had learned the true sound German honour and modesty, and when he came under the influence of Gerbert he had built up the designs of a universal reformation based on his empire. Gerbert, besides being a scholar, was a deep thinking and fearless politician, a fit director for the young knight-errant, as we might think him, who was to go out to renew the golden age. Rome was to be the capital and seat of the empire; Rome was to be purged of all the vices and crimes that had cried out so long for the punishment of Sodom. The wicked priests and abandoned nobles were to be made to give place to an apostolic company of holy fathers and a gallant court of true faithful heroes. It was not to be a mere vision either: deep political contrivance, unswerving honesty and force of purpose, were there as well as high imagination. The corruption of Rome must be rooted out; life must be put into all that was good that remained; that which was rotten must perish. The romantic love of Otto was given to his ideal Rome, the mother of the Churches, the queen of the world.

The Coronation of Otto at Rome, 996.—The early feuds of the reign having been settled by the victories of Otto and his generals, the danger of hostility from France being ended by the final displacement of the Karolings by Hugh Capet, and the power of Otto in Germany itself being universally accepted, in the year 996 Otto made his first expedition to Rome. John XV., in the midst of his struggle with Crescentius, had invited him two years before to come and receive the imperial crown; but the young king was too wise to leave Germany whilst the Slavs were ravaging the frontier. Nor had he yet got from Gerbert the political lessons which were to make the way practical to his noble ambition. Gerbert had been the friend and correspondent of Queen Adelheid, but had of late been estranged from the imperial court. For on the death of Lewis, the last of the Karoling kings of France, and on the deposition of Arnulf, Archbishop of Rheims, the earnest partizan of that house, he had suffered himself to be placed in the primatial see by the influence of Hugh Capet. The Karoling interest was still understood to be under the protection of the German kings, who had tolerated and supported them so long; and the Empress Adelheid, herself took up the cause of Arnulf. Gerbert, too independent a man to be a tool of any policy, was condemned and interdicted in a council of bishops held at Soissons in 995. He then retired from France and devoted himself to Otto. With him for his chief adviser the young king the next year started for Italy, intending to crush the republicanism and other hydra-headed abominations of Rome and realise his dream. He was but sixteen years old now, and if we find fault with him, his age must excuse him. With a great host of counts and bishops he crossed the Alps; he kept Easter at Pavia; at Ravenna he heard of the death of the Pope John XV. (985–996), and there he determined to place his cousin Bruno, son of Otto, Duke of Franconia, upon the papal throne. Bruno was sent on in advance, and was received by the Romans under the name of Gregory V. (996–999). Otto followed him, and was crowned emperor on the 21st of May 996. Crescentius was summoned before him, but was pardoned at the request of the Pope, whom, as soon as the emperor had left, he expelled from Rome. Otto, having received an oath of fealty to himself and the Pope, returned in September to Germany.

Second Visit to Italy, 998.—Whether Otto's return was to resist a new invasion of the Slavs, or to take measures for a future visit to Italy which should be permanent, it is difficult to determine; but the year

997 was spent in the reduction of this obstinate enemy, and it was not until the end of it that Otto was able again to be on the move. In the meantime Crescentius had expelled Bruno from Rome; had placed John Philagathus, a Greek and an old favourite of the Empress Theophanô, on the papal chair, and had himself taken the title of emperor. The Germans believed that Rome was to be permanently withdrawn from their dominion and restored to the Byzantine emperors, whose viceroy Crescentius would willingly be. This touched the very root of Otto's favourite scheme; he committed Germany to his aunt Matilda, the Abbess of Quedlinburg, a lady who seems to have inherited the spirit and ability of Otto the Great, and hastened into Italy in the depth of winter. In January 998 he reached Pavia; in February, with Gregory V. in his train, he advanced upon Rome; no resistance was offered him. He deposed the antipope, who was cruelly mutilated and ill-treated by his austere rival; and Crescentius, after surrendering the castle of St. Angelo, was hanged with his head downwards. Otto remained for more than a year in Italy on this occasion. In the February of 999 Gregory V. died, poisoned, it was said, by the Crescentian party, and Gerbert, whom in 998 he had made a Bishop of Ravenna, the emperor now made Pope. He took the name of Sylvester II., intending doubtless, as Milman reminds us, to be the new Sylvester of the new Constantine.

Otto's Return to Germany, 999.—On his return to Germany, Otto went through two ceremonial observances which are significant in his case. He went to Gnesen in Poland on pilgrimage to the scene of the martyrdom of St. Adalbert, who had died there four years before. The Church itself he raised into an archiepiscopal see, and erected three others as suffragans to it. The Duke of Poland, Boleslaus, he entrusted with the guardianship of the frontier against the Slavs, and according to the Polish historians allowed to be crowned king. He then went to Aix-la-Chapelle and held a diet there, at which he opened the grave of the great Charles, and took out the golden cup which was hung to his neck. There, the historians tell us, he showed his wish to adopt the imperial state and pomp, sitting alone at a semicircular table on a high daïs.

Otto's Last Visit to Italy 1000, *and Death*, 1002.—In October 1000 he was again at Rome. The transactions of these latter days are not clear ; but it is plain that the emperor had thrown himself, with too little reserve, on the good faith of the Romans, and had not retained force enough with him to keep order. Instead of being able to initiate a new reign of order, he found himself involved in petty squabbles, and obliged to treat by means of envoys with his own subjects. In February 1001 he left Rome with the Pope and spent the next few months in attempting to produce a better understanding. Otto did not die at Rome, but on January 23, 1002, at Paterno, near Civita Castellana : his body was embalmed and carried to Aix-la-Chapelle, where it was buried. With him the descendants of Otto the Great in the male line ended. Such was the sad conclusion, at the age of twenty-one, of a life full of so bright hopes—a prince of such noble gifts and accomplishments, so pious, so virtuous, so high-minded, at the head of a realm so united, surrounded by followers so faithful and undivided—a life such as the Middle Ages had never seen. Charles the Great was an old man before he obtained anything like peace, or time for legislation

and study; Otto, *mirabilia mundi*, the wonder of the
world for wisdom, eloquence, prudence, and high
enterprise, at the age when other princes are putting
on their arms first, died full of glory. The grief of
the German empire left without such a ruler can well
be understood. Gerbert survived him for about a
year and a half, and then the Romans poisoned him.
Otto's death took place on the 22nd of January 1002,
Sylvester's on the 12th of May 1003.

Condition of the Empire at the Time of Otto's Death.—
When Otto died Germany was enjoying profound peace.
The old sore about Lorraine with France was healed ;
the King of Arles was a faithful vassal of his kinsman ;
Italy, except Rome itself, was at peace and likely to
remain so. Byzantium was not likely to stir; Otto
was nephew of the emperors Basil and Constantine,
and in treaty for a Grecian empress. Poland was
organised and tributary; the Hungarians had received
in the year 1000 a crown from the Pope for their
Apostolic King Stephen, under whom they were Christianised permanently. It is impossible to think Otto
irrationally sanguine, if he did dream of a restored
empire, the seat of which should be Old Rome. But
Rome, after every cleansing, was reoccupied by seven
spirits more wicked than the first, and the last state
is ever worse than the former. Rome, the object of
Otto's peculiar love, was the one exception when all
besides loved him. And Rome was his destruction.[1]

Henry II. Emperor, 1002-1024.—Notice has already
been taken of Henry the Quarrelsome the first and
his son, Henry the Quarrelsome the second. The
first, a younger son of Henry the Fowler, was made

---

[1] I have dwelt on him thus long because I do not think that Milman, with
all his admiration for him, does him justice.

Duke of Bavaria by his brother, Otto I.; he married Judith, a Bavarian princess, daughter of Duke Arnulf; and was himself a constant rebel and divider of the strength of the imperial house. And notice has also been taken of his son, Henry the Quarrelsome II., the rival of Otto II., and kidnapper of Otto III. How hard these men had striven, first to separate Bavaria from the German kingdom, then to separate the German kingdom from the empire; then to divide the allegiance of the Saxons! Now they are dead, Henry II. in 995; and the representation of Henry the Fowler and his Saxon and Bavarian descendants centres in another Henry, who is not Quarrelsome III., but Saint Henry, the father of the monks, also called the Glorious and the Lame; a sad sick prince troubled with many diseases, but a good prince and popular upon the whole. It is satisfactory to know that his father had repented heartily on his deathbed, and given him the best advice; also that the pious son had taken it. The question of succession was not clear. Poor Otto, in the pain and misery of his sickness, had left no clear recommendation about the succession. According to one story he had commended the Royal Insignia to Herbert, Archbishop of Cologne, to be conveyed to his brother-in-law, the Count Palatine Ezzo, but it was not clear whether it was as to the official trustee of the regalia or as to the presumptive heir. On the other hand, Duke Henry, who had been with Otto in Italy, had, as his nearest relation, taken charge of his funeral. And Henry was the candidate who met with most favour, although Hermann of Swabia united many votes. The diet was held at Werle in Westphalia (Lower Saxony), and there, by the influence of Bernard Billung, Duke of Saxony,

and Dietrich of Lorraine, greatly supported by the
clergy, Henry was chosen king, and to him was committed the sacred lance of Constantine which, since
the days of Henry the Fowler, had been the most
precious of the imperial treasures. The ceremony of
election was transacted at Mainz on the 6th of June,
and Henry was forthwith anointed and crowned. The
ceremony was repeated a few days after at Aix. He
reigned for twenty-two years.

His Wars with the Bohemians, the Poles, and Flanders.
—The new king was as usual welcomed with a little
rebellion; in which his brother Bruno, Bishop of
Augsburg, a very young man, and Hezelo or Henry
Junior, the son of Berthold, joined. But both this and
the short resistance offered him by Duke Hermann of
Swabia, seem to have been movements originated by
mere restlessness and personal ambition, taking the
opportunity from the yet untried and reported weakness of Henry. The king was strong enough not
only to conquer but to pardon them, although they
had done their worst by attempting to draw the
Bohemians into their quarrel. The wars with Bohemia
spread over more than twelve years of the reign; they
are very uninteresting and tedious, but serve to show
the hand of the German king gaining gradually a
firmer hold on the Slavonic countries. A new mark
on the Elbe was created by Henry against the Slavs
and Bohemians, and his wars with Poland and the
Northern Slavs seem to have been equally successful.
His home management was good. His wife, Cunigunda, was a daughter of Sigfrid, Count of Luxemburg,
and a lady of great piety and influence. To her Henry
allowed a great deal of authority; had her specially
crowned at Paderborn soon after his own accession,

and bestowed his duchy of Bavaria on Henry, her brother, in 1004. The same year rid him of his rival, Hermann of Swabia, whom he replaced by a second Hermann, son of the first; and the next year he was able to put a man of his own into Lorraine. His sister Gisela was married to Stephen, the apostolic King of Hungary. Unfortunately as usual the family party did not agree, and the king was obliged to resume the duchy of Bavaria for several years; but Henry was subsequently restored and continued faithful. He had probably done little more than justify his right to the confidence of the Bavarians by attempting to make them again an independent nation. A more significant transaction is the war with Baldwin, Count of Flanders, which occurred in the year 1006; and which shows the rising power of that important county, destined in after ages so greatly to affect both Germany and France, and in the person of Charles V. to overshadow all Europe. Baldwin had seized Valenciennes, which was on the border of the imperial dominions, the march of Antwerp. The emperor invaded, Flanders, and after some difficulties compelled Baldwin to submit; but, perceiving the desirableness of making him a friend, he subsequently gave him the place and a handsome fief with it. In 1005 he bestowed the duchy of Lower Lorraine upon Godfrey, Count of the Ardennes, under whose posterity it continued to be held, not without occasional changes, as a benefice for nearly a century.

Connection of England with Lorraine and Flanders.— The period is interesting as being that of the closest intercourse between England and Lorraine, which filled the sees of Wessex with Lotharingian bishops, and introduced or rather failed to acclimatise the Lothar-

ingian rule of canons to the air of the English cathe-
drals. Very noticeable also is the close connection
between the courts of Flanders and England under
both Ethelred II. and Canute, as illustrated by the
marriage of Tostig, the son of Godwin, with the
daughter of the Count of Flanders, and the protection received by that house when in exile at St.
Omer. Nor should it be forgotten that it is with the
Emperor Henry II. and Stephen, King of Hungary,
his brother-in-law, that the sons of Edmund Ironside
find refuge, and that to a niece of the emperor Edward
the Atheling is married.

Henry II.'s Visits to Italy, 1004 *and* 1013.—With the
exception of one important measure upon which something will be said later, the remaining interest of
Henry II.'s reign lies in Italy. One of the great
measures of Otto III. had been to bind the Romans,
so far as they could be bound, to an agreement that
the person on whom for the future the suffrages of
the Germans should fall, should be received by the
Romans as King of the Germans, and forthwith consecrated emperor. The fact that such an agreement
had been made was a great inducement to break
through it; and accordingly, as soon as Otto was
dead, the Italians chose themselves a king, Ardoin,
Marquis of Ivrea. The Italian bishops, however, resisted this election, and meeting with severe treatment
from Ardoin in consequence, had recourse immediately
to Henry for assistance. He forthwith sent Otto, the
Duke of Franconia, into Lombardy in the year 1002,
and, finding him successful against Ardoin, followed
in person in 1004. In this expedition he took Verona
and Brescia and burned Pavia, but was notwithstanding crowned there as King of Italy. From this

time for the next seven years a languid sort of war
was carried on between Henry and Ardoin, the advantage being chiefly with the former.   In 1012, Pope
Benedict VIII. implored Henry's assistance, and even
came to him in Germany to persuade him to make
an effort to win the imperial crown.   Henry was not
proof against the prayers and promises of a Pope;
in 1013, he started at the head of a large army.
Ardoin, at his approach, sent in his submission entreating to be provided for by the gift of some county
by way of a fief; but Henry, supported by the bishops,
refused to do this, and Ardoin accordingly took up
arms, seized Vercelli, Novara, and Como.   Henry,
however, was much more than a match for him;
by one lucky stroke he took prisoners four Italian
marquises, who were the chief supporters of Ardoin,
retook Vercelli, and reduced Ardoin to complete in-
digence.   He took refuge in a monastery, deposited
his royal robes on the altar, and remained there himself in sanctuary until his death in 1015.   In this
little episode of Italian life, far more interesting than
all the disputes at Rome about the candidates for the
Papacy, can be traced a considerable growth of that
spirit which was to make Italy impossible for the
Germans, and which was seen in the springing up of
a native aristocracy in Lombardy and Piedmont, under
whose protection the cities were sooner or later to
spring up to vigorous life.   The names are still for
the most part German in origin but being softened
down into Italian, a sure token of the incorporation
of the nobles, once German or Frank officials, into
the mass of the Latin-speaking people.   Ardoin was
a Lombard hero, as his opponents were German and
imperialised bishops.

Coronation of Henry at Rome, 1014—*His Third Visit to Italy,* 1022.—After the conquest of Ardoin, Henry followed Benedict to Rome, and there, after some little reluctance on the Pope's part, he was crowned emperor on the 14th of February 1014; Queen Cunigunda was crowned empress with him. It was, however, only a tame proceeding. Although Henry coined money at Rome as emperor, and administered justice in person, the Pope, who had a strong party at Rome, maintained a very independent position; and although on friendly terms with the emperor, treated with him as an equal, which Henry's pious humility was well able to tolerate. This same Pope Benedict reigned until 1024, and was quite equal to his position temporally; he roused up the Pisans to drive the Saracens out of Italy, and was on the whole a very vigorous Pope. In 1022, Henry at his invitation made another expedition to Italy, intended to subdue Apulia and Calabria, where the Greek empire was again showing signs of life. He descended with a great army, defeated the Greeks, and took several cities. But the occasion is chiefly memorable as that on which the presence of the Normans in Apulia was first formally recognised. Henry bestowed, according to Hermann Contractus, some lands upon them in this expedition. They were probably mere adventurers who had taken service with him as their brethren were ready to do with the Greeks of Naples or the Saracens of Bari; but from this little seed sprang first the little State of Aversa, and after it the goodly tree of the Sicilian kingdom, so fatally affecting the empire and Germany itself in the history of Frederick II., Conrad, and Conradin. On his return from this expedition Henry suffered greatly from the heat of Rome and the Campania, and hastened back into Germany. One of his last acts was to make a treaty with Robert, King of France, in which all disputes between the kingdoms were arranged. Henry had already been declared heir of the kingdom of Arles, but he did not live to claim it. After calling a council, at which he nominated Conrad the Salic to be his successor, he died at Grun in Saxony on the 14th of July 1024.

Henry's Death, 1024, *and Character.*—There can be no doubt that he was a very good prince, and that Germany enjoyed peace and good government under him. Although not a warrior and physically incapacitated for much exertion, he showed himself vigorous on occasion, and experienced fewer defeats either in war or policy than his predecessors. In some respects he resembles Edward the Confessor, but the comparison must be to the advantage of Henry. Take him altogether he seems to have been a quiet, pious, and honest prince ; his character as a saint, which was not fully recognised until nearly two centuries after his death, may have been founded rather on his supposed possession of the virtues attributed to Edward the Confessor, than on his actual merits. Still he was a great temporal benefactor to the Church : a great founder and reformer, and the first of. the German kings who had taken a pride in being so. Otto the Great and Henry the Fowler had spread the influence of Christianity, divided sees and founded churches for the consolidation and evangelising of the kingdom ; but Henry was the first who, by his munificent or rather lavish outlay on the Church, seemed to be laying up a stock of merits without any other determinate object. Yet in this point, in which he comes nearest to Edward the Confessor (for what Westminster was to Edward, Bamberg was to Henry), we see the difference of character. Westminster was but a monastery, although one of unparalleled beauty and wealth ; Bamberg was a strong bishopric and principality, able to succour the empire with arms and counsel as well as to pray for the souls of himself and Cunegunda.

Henry's Relations with the German Church. — This foundation of Bamberg is the typical act of Henry's reign, and illustrates his Church policy. Henry's benefactions were, however, by no means confined to Bamberg, but all the great churches of the kingdom were largely indebted to him ; and he seems to have taken a pleasure in being enrolled on the lists of the monks or canons as a sort of honorary member thus entitled to the benefit of their prayers and alms. In one case he is said to have prevailed on an abbot to admit him as a monk, but, as soon as he had taken the vow of obedience, the abbot commanded him to return and resume the empire, not to part with it until his death. But this story, which is said to have happened at Verdun, Strassburg, and Monte Casino, is not likely to be true. The history of the Bamberg foundation was as follows. The Counts of Bamberg had been turbulent in the reign of Henry the Fowler, had disputed the duchy of Franconia with Conrad I., and were subsequently provided for by Henry with the Margraviate of Austria. On the forfeiture of Count Adalbert, Bamberg had been given either by Henry or Otto I. to Henry the Quarrelsome I. of Bavaria, as a piece of private property ; from him it descended to his grandson the Emperor Henry II., and he devoted it to the foundation of a bishopric. The diocese was cut out of the diocese of Würzburg, and the magnificent church was built in which Henry and Cunigunda still lie. This church was privileged to be subject to no

I

metropolitan, or to any human superior but the Pope of Rome ; it was endowed with estates in several remote parts of the empire ; and, as a peculiar privilege, the four great dukes were enjoined to perform, to the bishops, the same services of Grand Serjeanty that they performed to the emperor :[1]—the Duke of Saxony as marshal, the Duke of Bavaria as steward, the Margrave of Brandenburg as chamberlain, and the King of Bohemia as cup-bearer. The subjection of the bishop to Rome was to be expressed in the gift of 100 marks of silver and a white horse annually to the Pope, but this was exchanged by the Emperor Henry III. for the town of Benevento, which ever after that belonged to the Popes.

The Ecclesiastical Organisation of the German States.— The processes by which the different states of Germany had been ecclesiastically organised have often been mentioned. We saw that the dioceses or archbishoprics of Cologne, Mainz, and Trier were of the Gallo-Roman foundation ; that the Franconian as well as the Alemannian churches sprang up under the Merovingian kings, the Bavarian about the beginning of the seventh century on the conversion of Theudo. The Westphalian dioceses were created by Charles the Great ; the rest of those of Saxony, Denmark, and the march of Brandenburg, with some in Bohemia, by Otto the Great ; those of Poland and Hungary by the advice or more determinate action of Otto III. All these sees were apportioned to the older and more dignified churches as suffragans, the province of Mainz being far the larger ; Bavaria was subject to the Archbishop of Salzburg, and the Slav churches and marches to the north-east to Magdeburg. Westphalia was given

---

[1] The story of the Grand Serjeanty is very apocryphal.

to the Archbishop of Cologne as its spiritual head. Amongst these, however, the three archbishops on the Rhine succeeded in getting the most political power into their hands, as might be expected. Especially under Otto the Great they received both titles and privileges. The Archbishop of Mainz became Archchancellor of the empire, that of Cologne, Archchancellor of Italy, and that of Trier, Archchancellor of Burgundy. But this must have been later than Otto's time, probably in the eleventh century after the kingdom of Arles fell into the empire. Otto did, however, greatly augment the power of the archbishops, to whom he is said to have given Hesse and Thuringia, which were afterwards held by the Landgraves as a fief under the archbishops; but this is thought to be an invention of later times, and is not mentioned by the contemporary historians. A more substantial gain was the acquisition of secular rights over the domains of their churches. From the Karoling rulers it was common for the prelates to obtain for their tenants exemption from the jurisdiction of the secular officers of the empire and from imposts and taxes payable to them. Upon this basis they erected their own courts, coined their own money, and held and regulated their own markets; a further step was to accept the offices of secular jurisdiction over other territories and join them to their sees. Mosheim fixes this to the tenth century, and probably it is to Otto the Great that we are to ascribe the common introduction of the grant of regalia to the bishops and archbishops; meaning by the word, the right of coining, of jurisdiction, and of fortifying their own castles. To distinct gifts of such privileges and to the distinct extension of the immediate jurisdiction of prelates by the gifts of new estates, can be ascribed the difference of the positions of the German prelates in the diets of the empire. As a rule the more ancient the See, the nearer the Rhine, the greater the privileges. But they did not spring up at once; they were the result of accumulations and of pretensions ever on the increase. An attempt has already been made to point out how they were created. The leaven of the old Gallo-Roman secularism in the Rhenish Churches was one cause; the growth of Christianity under the Imperial system was another; a third was the entrance by the prelates upon the escheated and forfeited estates of the counts and barons, and their secular acquisitions made by war, purchase, and exchange after their position as secular as well as ecclesiastical princes was recognised.

Summary.—Of great interest then is the history of the conversion of Germany, of the acquisition of regalia by the prelates, and of the improvement of their secular position by the acquisition of territory. What advantages the prelates have secured under the Ottos were confirmed and strengthened under Henry II. Each prelate was, like the Pope of Rome, getting a little temporal principality quite distinct from his diocesan or provincial jurisdiction; and to this he sometimes added, as the Archduke Bruno did to his jurisdiction as archbishop, the administration of an imperial duchy or even more than one. Of course this increased considerably after the fall of the great houses, and still more after the humiliation and long abeyance of the empire. The growth of the German Church is comparable to nothing else in Europe except the Papacy; but now the Papacy was subject to the empire much as the prince bishops were. The time was coming when it would vindicate for itself a superior claim and meet its stoutest opponents in these very prelates.

IMPORTANT DATES

Coronation of Otto at Rome, 996.
Otto's second visit to Rome, 998.
Otto in Germany, 999.
His third visit to Italy, 1000.
His death, 1002.
Henry II. Emperor, 1002-1024.
Wars with Poland, 1003-1017.
Henry visits Italy, 1004.
Coronation of Henry at Rome, 1014.
The Pope visits Henry at Bamberg, 1020.
Henry wars against the Greeks in the South of Italy, 1021.

CHAPTER VIII

England and Germany compared—Development of feudalism in
England, Germany, and France—Conrad the Salic, 1024–1039—
Conrad visits Italy—Coronation at Rome—The Edict making
fiefs hereditary, 1037—Changes in the great Duchies—Henry III.,
1039–1056—Characteristics of the English, French, and German
nations.

*The Condition of England and Germany in the early Years of
the Tenth Century compared.*—The increasing light which
we now begin to have with reference to the internal
administration of Germany, coming at a time when for
England also both our historians, laws, and *corpus
diplomaticum* are so much fuller than they have been,
seems to invite a comparison between the conditions
of the two countries so near akin in blood and institutions. Both kingdoms were composed of several
minor states which had become subject about the
same time to a central authority. The year 800, which
marks the acquisition of the empire by Charles the
Great, marks the accession of Egbert, who was to unite
all the kingdoms of the English under the supremacy
of Wessex ; in both countries great drawbacks to centralisation and civilisation had been experienced by the
invasion of barbarians ; within a very few years England
was desolated by the Danes and Germany by the Hungarians ; within a very few years also the same date
might do for the termination of these ravages, the
Hungarians being finally defeated by Otto in 955, and
the Danes firmly kept down in England by Athelstan
and his immediate successors. In both countries, both

now and long after, the different tribal divisions had their distinct codes of law; the West Saxon, Mercian, and Danish law in England, answer to the Alemannian, Bavarian, and Saxon laws in Germany. Each kingdom stood in a sort of feudal superiority to neighbour kingdoms. Putting aside the Imperial Theory, what Germany was to Bohemia, Denmark, and Burgundy, England was to Scotland and the kingdom of Strath Clyde. By commendation the inferior kings had made themselves the vassals of the superior. Nor should we carry our parallel further than we are warranted in doing, if we compared the marches of Wales with those of the Wends, Slavs, and Obotrites in Germany. Nearly at the same time the ecclesiastical constitution of the two countries had been completed. Edward the elder filled up the tale of bishoprics by his new foundations in 909, just as Otto the Great was doing in Germany thirty years later. In both countries the remnants of the rival dynasties, which had been compelled to yield submission to the superior state, remained for a long time to prevent perfect union and to give a gathering point for discontent.

Points of Similarity and Dissimilarity in Principles of Government.—Almost all the fundamental principles of government and administration were the same, derived and with little difference of growth as yet from the old Teutonic model. Such were the divisions of the country, the character of jurisdictions, the distinct judicial peculiarities of process; the weregild, the compurgatory oath, the periodical meetings of the district, the central *placita*, secular, religious, and military; the names of the officers differing, but the reality corresponding—the earl or ealdorman answering to the duke or herzog; the *scygerefa* or sheriff to the graf or count; the centenarius to the headman of the hundred; the German duchy to the Anglo-Saxon sub-kingdom; and possibly or approximately their gau to our shire. Against these points of similarity we shall have to set several points in which the condition of Germany is to be contrasted with that of England.

1. *Difference in Size.*—The first and most obvious is that of size. England is fitted, as an island and by its extent, to be a compact country; Germany is so large as to be unwieldy. With the size comes the diversity of nationality. The several nations of Germany had had a history, a distinct history each of its own, before they became one. But the Anglo-Saxons had no national existence before they became English; at the best their history was tribal, at the worst it was merely the adventures of companies of colonists emigrating from their country in conjunction. Bavaria was a nation before it came a part of the Frank empire; Wessex not only was not a nation but the West Saxons were only a division of a larger nation, other divisions of which colonised the country about them.

2. *Different System of Development.*—Secondly, Germany was conquered and civilised by the arms of the Franks, but England was civilised before it was united under the sway of Wessex. Germany was conquered before it was Christianised. England was Christianised before it was consolidated. Germany became Christian because it was united, and it was Christianised by union; England was united by Christianity. In England the Church framework preceded the union of the empire; in Germany it followed it.

3. *No Roman Element in England.*—In the third place, Germany was from the beginning leavened with a Roman element from which England was free, and

which of course assumed far greater proportions after the Imperial dignity was sealed to Germany, first under Charles the Great and secondly under Otto. The Rhine provinces of Germany had been under Roman laws for centuries ; Alemannia had formed the *Agri Decumates* of the Roman empire ; the south of Bavaria had been included in a Roman province ; it is only of Saxony that we can distinctly say that the Romans had had no direct hand in the making it what it was. The Franks themselves were the most Romanised of the German nations ; before the time of Clovis they had fought on the side of the Romans. Clovis was proud to be regarded as a Roman officer. Brunechild and her family were in close alliance with Rome, and had very Roman ideas of government. Charles the Great, although too wise a man to dream of applying the principles of Imperial despotism, was not averse to adopting the pomp and style of Imperial Rome, and the shadows of old realities into which a bold hand might yet put life. The conjunction of this aggregate of Roman influences with the substratum of German institutions common to the whole race, was the origin of feudalism ; but under Charles the Great the feudal system as a system of government was still a long way off, and the perfecting of it as a system of land tenure belongs to the reign of Conrad the Salic. But the most efficacious influence of Roman Imperialism was imported by the incorporating of the claims upon Italy with the imperial character of the German king, and the constant association subsisting thenceforth between two countries in other respects so much divided.

4. *No Difficulty in England in Conciliating various Races under one King.*—Fourthly, the reason of disunion and disaffection in England proceeded not from the im-

possibility of conciliating hostile races under the sway of one king, nor from the power of hereditary dynasts building a dynastic insubordination or independence on the combination between national antipathies and hereditary ambitions; for in England there was no such national or tribal antipathy, and there was as yet no hereditary chieftainship approaching the character of a German duchy or a French county. For we must compare England with both. In France the provincial rulers had become *ipso facto* hereditary; in Germany they were from time to time bestowed on the son in succession to the father, but with nothing more than a presumption of right; the gift by the emperor was a new gift to each new possessor. In England the ealdormanships were not so near the hereditary type as that, although, as in Germany, as a matter of grace or convenience, the son might often succeed the father. Doubtless the same tendency was observable in England, and it did come to the same point under the preponderating influence of the two great houses of Leofric and Godwin, and so opened the way to the Norman Conquest. Still, even if the likeness in this respect were really greater than it seems to me to have been, the divisions of the provinces being based on no radical distinction of nationality, or on such as were long ago obsolete, prevented the disruption of England into petty states such as Germany was in constant risk of breaking up into.

Lastly, it is impossible to doubt, however highly you may estimate the progress towards a feudal tenure of land which had been made in England before the Norman Conquest by the practice of commendation, by the division of great estates and by the distribution of the public lands, supposing that to have taken place, that the system had made much greater progress in Germany than in England, as it had made more in France than in Germany. We ascribed the growth of the system in France, as compared with its growth in Germany, to the earlier civilisation and to the measure of admixture of Frank Lords with native tenants. In Germany we did not see the same predominance of Frank nobles, the native nobles being left in their old allodial position. Still the close alliance with the Franks, the fact that they were so long the leading if not throughout the dominant race, and the natural working towards centralisation under Frank imperialism, quickened the growth and spread the system far more than anything that can be shown to have existed in England. With a feudal land-tenure there is a strong impulse towards a feudal provincial government, that is towards ultimate disruption. Thus feudal government in England and Germany was based upon two different principles. With so much by way of preface we are prepared for the conclusion.

The Development of Feudalism in England, France, and Germany.—There are stages in the life of a country when feudalism is a source of strength, and others when it is a source of weakness; much depends on the character of the central government, much on the character of the feudalism itself. At this point the feudalism of France was the cause of its impotency; that of Germany the cause or expression of its strength. In England the case was entirely different. The Norman Conquest was a solution of the continuous development of the feudal principle in England, however we might have been advancing towards it; the system that followed the Norman Conquest did not grow out of the system that prevailed before it, it

came in *per saltum*, and we can never say to what the
elder system, left to itself, might or might not have
brought us. Most of the points already alluded to
will be seen illustrated in the epoch on which we
have now to enter, that of the Franconian Empire,
which extends from the election of Conrad the Salic
in 1024 to the death of Henry V. in 1125—a period
of history which contains the point of greatest exaltation, and also of the greatest humiliation, experienced
by the German emperors before the fall of Frederick
II. The flourishing period of the empire may be
divided according to the nationality of the province
which gave the dynasty, a nationality often not the
same as that of the dynasty itself, but strong enough
in all the cases to give some colour to the politics
of it. Thus we get first the Saxon, then the Franconian, and finally the Alemannian or Swabian period ;
they run into one another by a succession but little
removed from hereditary, but still the fact that the
imperial connections and influence lay in different
nations gives a warrant for the political as well as
the mere memorial usefulness of the division. The
Bavarian nation struggles continuously through the
first and third of the dynasties ; through the Ottos,
under the Quarrelsome Henrys, and through the
Hohenstaufens, in the person of the Welfic Henrys.
But Bavaria never gets a firm hold on the imperial
crown, and indeed the Welfic interest lay rather in
Saxony than in Bavaria itself. The house of Austria,
however, which comes in so much later, and the bulk
of whose German possessions lie within the ancient
Bavaria, may be considered as taking the Bavarian turn.

Conrad the Salic, 1024-1039.—Henry II. on his deathbed recommended as his successor Conrad the Salic.

Conrad was the male representative of that Conrad the Wise, Duke of Franconia, to whom Otto the Great gave his daughter Luitgarde. He was thus descended from our English Alfred, and is the first of the emperors who is so. He was the son of Henry, the son of Otto, the son of Conrad and Luitgarde. His father died during Duke Otto's lifetime, and so, although he was of age at his grandfather's death, he was not allowed to succeed to the duchy, but it was given to his uncle Conrad, on whose death his own son Conrad succeeded him; so that our Conrad, called the Salic by way of distinction, although the elder of the two, and representing the elder branch, was not Duke of Franconia. This then is the first case of an emperor being chosen who was not either the heir-apparent or in possession of one of the great national duchies. Conrad was chosen by the Germans on the strength of his cousin's recommendation, about six weeks after his death, in a diet at Kamb, between Mainz and Worms, attended by representatives of all the nations, and was crowned at Mainz on the 14th of September 1024. The life of Conrad is extant, written by his chaplain Wippo in a very excellent and workmanlike book. He begins with an account of the *dramatis personæ*, and the names of the bishops and dukes. Of the latter he names eight: the four of the great nations, Conrad of Franconia, Henry of Bavaria, Ernest of Alemannia, and Bernard Billung of Saxony; the two of Lorraine, Frederick of Lower and Gozelo of Upper or Ripuarian Lorraine; Adalbero, Duke of Istria, and Ulric, Duke of Bohemia. Istria had been held sometimes with Franconia and sometimes with Bavaria; just now and for a short time it was a separate duchy. The Count Palatine does not yet come out as a prince; his position

was greatly enhanced by the abeyance of the duchy
of Franconia which took place under this dynasty.
After a long description of the election and coronation
of Conrad, Wippo tells us about the Empress Gisela,
who was sister of Duke Ernest of Alemannia, and
ought to have kept her brother and husband at peace.
She was not a popular lady although worthy, rather
interfering, we may conclude, and her coronation was
impeded for some days, taking place at Cologne on
the 21st of September.

Conrad visits Italy.—This done, Conrad, in accordance
with ancient precedent, made a tour of his dominions,
going first to Aix-la-Chapelle and through the Ripuarian
duchy ; then into Saxony, where he confirmed the strict
Saxon laws ; so to Bavaria, then to Franconia, and
ending the circuit in Alemannia. Having thus visited
Germany, he went into Italy in the next spring, and
there reconciled the Italians, who had as usual broken
out at the news of Henry's death and burned the palace
of Pavia ;[1] receiving the submission of the Lombards
at Milan but rejecting the apology of Pavia, and waiting
for an opportunity of exacting severe punishment. He
returned by way of Swabia to Zurich and Basel, where
he exercised the right of appointing a bishop, although
it was in the kingdom of Burgundy, not without a stain
of simony, of which he lived to repent. The next year,
having designated his son Henry, now quite a child, as
his successor and entrusted him to the care of Bishop
Bruno of Augsburg, Conrad marched into Italy, partly
with a view of punishing the people of Pavia and partly
intending to demand the imperial crown. Already some
discontent was showing itself in Germany. Duke Ernest

---

[1] They had tried to join in electing the King of France or William of
Aquitaine.

of Alemannia, Conrad of Franconia, and Frederick of
Lorraine were, according to the tradition of their
ancestors, preparing for a rebellion. Conrad, however,
thought light of them and carried off Ernest with him
in his army to Italy, when he redeemed his fault for
the time by his generalship. Pavia had to pay heavily
for the offence of last year, and Italy, or Lombardy
generally, experienced the severe justice of Conrad.
From the language in which Wippo describes these
measures we may conclude that the country about
Pavia was entirely desolated, churches and castles de-
molished, commerce forbidden, and entire submission
enforced by the grinding discipline of two years of
punishment. Conrad spent nearly a year in Italy,
staying at Ravenna in the winter and going to the
Apennines in the hot weather.

Coronation at Rome, 1027.—At last, on Easter day
1027, he was crowned with his wife at Rome in the
presence of Rudolph of Burgundy and Canute, King
of England, who attended him on the occasion to his
chamber. Rudolph, of course, held his kingdom of the
empire, but if there were anything of the nature of
serjeanty implied in this attendance by Canute it must
have been in consideration of the kingdom of Denmark,
which had been commended to the emperor, or of some
other fief; for the territory of Schleswig was not yet,
nor until the year 1036, bestowed on the King of
Denmark as a fief. It is not uninteresting to observe
how early this question of Schleswig emerges, which
has given occasion to one of the greatest revolutions
of modern times within our own recollection; nor is
it less interesting to observe that at this very moment
the Bavarian Welfs are rising into importance, destined
to place themselves amongst the most prominent princes

of Europe, a position retained by them through many changes of fortune down to the time of the Prussian usurpation of Hanover in 1866.

The Later Years of Conrad's Reign.—It is curious to observe the smallness of the armies with which these long expeditions of the German sovereigns were made; neither Otto III. nor Henry II., nor again Conrad the Salic, seems to have led an army sufficiently large to keep order in Ravenna or Rome. Regularly, after the coronation of the emperor, a riot seems to have taken place in Rome, the result of which is scarcely creditable to the imperial power of keeping order. But it would seem that the state of the country was such that the Italians had no spirit for pertinacious resistance. The townspeople had spirit enough for riot, which their cruelty and passion generally made bloody; but, as for the country, it must be concluded either that the Germans with all their severity were welcome as bringing a moment's security and law with them, or else that the people had been too long disused to arms to resist them. From Rome Conrad went into Apulia, where he destroyed the power of Thasselgard, a great brigand leader, and hanged him. There also he gave authority to the Normans to colonise, and laid the foundations of the principality which was to rescue the Pope from imperial influence. He was, however, now recalled into Germany by the revival of the conspiracy of Ernest, Conrad, and Frederick, and by a private war between Count Welf of Altdorf and Bishop Bruno of Augsburg. The war as usual collapsed at the emperor's appearance. Rudolf of Burgundy checked the ravages of Ernest, and his own followers deserted him. Adalbero, Duke of Carinthia, was deprived and exiled, and Conrad of Franconia, receiving that dukedom in addition to his own, repented of his treason and continued ever after faithful to his cousin. Peace being restored, Henry, the son of Conrad, now eleven years old, was crowned at Aix-la-Chapelle by the Archbishop of Cologne. The remaining events of the reign of Conrad, as Wippo relates them, are few : the release, renewed rebellion, and final forfeiture of Duke Ernest in the year 1030, and the gift of his duchy to his brother Hermann ; the falling in of the kingdom of Burgundy on Rudolf's death in 1032 ; the contest for it with Odo of Champagne, and the subsequent bestowal of it (together with the duchy of Alemannia on the death of Hermann) by Conrad on his son Henry ; the death of Bishop Bruno, the last of the Saxon family ; the marriage of Henry with Gunhilda, the daughter of Canute ; and some few tumults in Italy which called the emperor again into that country in 1036. On this occasion he visited Milan, where he published his famous enunciation of the feudal law, and Rome, where he restored Pope Benedict IX. After Christmas 1037, which he spent at Parma, he punished a revolt or riot of the inhabitants by burning the city; and he also enforced peace in Apulia with the strong hand. Wars with the Poles and Slavs make up the history of the reign. He died in 1039 at Utrecht, where he had been keeping Whitsuntide with great pomp. He was buried at Speyer, where he was building a cathedral which he destined for the burial-place of his family, and where his son, grandson, and great-grandson, the three Franconian Henrys, were buried.

Conrad's Character.—The character of Conrad is clearly that of a strong-handed, severe, and ready man. Much of his power was doubtless inherited from Henry II.; and in general he may be said to have succeeded to a sceptre very considerably strengthened by the

K

sway of the Saxon emperors. The power which Henry
the Fowler had founded, and Otto I. consolidated,
suffered no diminution before it reached him ; but
it is very much to his own personal qualities that we
are to attribute the facility with which he worked it,
and the equable pressure which he exercised by it, not
only through Germany but through the length and
breadth of Italy also. He was a strong man, if less
brilliant than Otto I. or Henry III.

The Edict making Fiefs Hereditary, 1037.—In another
point of view we get a glimpse of Conrad's powers
which makes us inclined to compare him with our
own Edward I., viz. in his enunciation of the feudal
law in the edict published by him on the Roman
expedition in the year 1037 at Milan. This edict has
been held to entitle him to be termed the first who
reduced the feudal law, strictly so called, to writing.
The essence of the feudal law had been hitherto, and
indeed its procedure always was, very much regulated
by custom ; but in this edict certain rules are laid
down which, by their soundness and universal application, gaining authority from the dignity of the pro-
mulgator, claimed and received universal acceptance.
Although in their immediate application they belonged
to Lombardy, we may be sure, from the words of
Wippo, (1) that, by approving the perpetuity of fiefs, he
gained the affection of his soldiers, (2) that they were
principles upon which in Germany also he acted in the
same matter. Hallam remarks that they show the
full maturity of the system and the last stage of its
progress.[1] By the system he means only the land
tenure of feudalism, for the governmental system and
most of the political phenomena which we usually

---

[1] See Hallam, " History of the Middle Ages," vol. i. p. 166.

associate under the name of the feudal system, were yet in an incipient stage in Germany.

The Rules laid Down in the Edict.—By the first of these he orders that no man shall be deprived of a fief whether held of the emperor or of a mesne lord, but by the laws of the empire and the judgment of his peers—an expression which is copied in our own Magna Carta, and which proves at once that the system of hereditary fiefs was now the customary rule, and that any infringement of it, however legitimate, on the original theory of feudalism, was now come to be regarded as unjust. Applying this to the distribution and continuance in one family of the great jurisdictions of the duchies, we see a reason for the patience and lenity with which the emperors treat their rebellious vassals. To have broken through such a custom, to have hastily exercised the right of confiscation or to have resumed a duchy at the death of its last holder, without regard to the rights of the heirs, would have set the whole body of feudatories in arms against him. The second article gives the immediate vassal or tenant-in-chief the right of appeal to the sovereign against the judgment of his peers. The third orders that fiefs shall be inherited by the sons and their children or, in their failure, by brothers, provided they were *feuda paterna* such as had descended from the father. By the fourth, it is ordered that the lord shall not alienate a fief without the consent of his vassal ; that he shall not transfer his own lordship over the fief without the consent of his tenant. The minutiæ of the question should be worked up by a careful reading of at least Hallam and Blackstone, and it may be added that in the reign of Otto the Great the right of representation had been allowed to grandchildren in the inheritance of their grandfathers; the question was tried by wager of battle and was so decided. But by this time the feudal law was hardly in such a state as to be affected by such a decision, most of the property heritable being still allodial; and the succession to the great fiefs was not regulated by it, as was seen in the case of Conrad himself, who otherwise would have been Duke of Franconia.

Changes in the Great Duchies in Conrad's Days.—The changes in the great duchies during the reign of Conrad the Salic were, with the exception of those which have been already noted, not very important. Saxony continued to be held by Bernard Billung, who governed it in all fifty-two years; Bavaria was governed by Henry of Luxemburg, a nephew of Queen Cunigunda, who was faithful all his life; Franconia we have accounted for under the history of Conrad; he died in 1039, and the duchy was given to the heir-apparent, Henry, who became king the same year. Lorraine was reunited in 1033 under Gothelo I., Duke of Lower Lorraine; and Alemannia, on the death of Hermann and Conrad, was given, like Franconia, to the young Henry, who was thus during his father's life put in possession of a compact territory comprising the kingdom of Arles and two of the great duchies of Germany. The year of the death of Conrad was marked, as Wippo tells us in his poem on the subject, by the loss to Germany of the Queen Gunhilda, wife of the young Henry, Conrad of Franconia, and many others. From this point a period of history is entered upon which has been written almost exclusively from an ecclesiastical standpoint; one way or the other all the writers on the Franconian empire have regarded it in its relations to the Papacy rather than in its relations to Germany.

Henry III., 1039–1056.—With regard to Henry III. there is no lack of interest from any point of view; he was one of the ablest, brightest, and strongest politicians of the Middle Ages; under him Germany reached its acme of consolidation and the empire its highest pitch of power. By way of preparation for the next chapter the principal dates of the reign and of Henry's life will now be given. Henry was born in the year 1017, and received Bavaria in 1026; crowned King of Germany in 1028; made Duke of Alemannia and Franconia and King of Arles in 1038; married first to Gunhilda, the daughter of Canute, King of England, who died in 1039, and secondly, to Agnes, daughter of William V., Duke of Aquitaine, in the year 1043; the latter was mother of the unfortunate King Henry IV. Henry III. reigned seventeen years and died in 1056. Lambert of Hersfeld, the historian of the next reign, gives a few dates and particulars of interest for this also. The early years of the reign were spent in Germany. His first visit to Italy was in 1046, when he deposed three popes, Benedict, Sylvester, and Gregory, and nominated a fourth, Clement II., before called Swidger, Bishop of Bamberg, who, on the day of his own coronation, bestowed the imperial crown on Henry and Agnes, Christmas day 1046. After visiting the South of Italy he returned to Germany. In 1047, on the death of Clement, he appointed, at the request of the Romans, Poppo, Bishop of Brixen, Pope under the title of Damasus II., and in 1048 he made in the same way Bruno, Bishop of Toul, Pope as Leo IX.; and in 1054, Gebhard of Eichstadt as Victor II. In 1055 he made his second Italian expedition to take measures for the humiliation of Godfrey, Duke of Lorraine, who had married the Countess Beatrice, widow of Boniface, Marquis of Tuscany, and mother by Boniface of the famous Countess Matilda. On this occasion he held a famous diet at Roncaglia, the plain on which the old Kings of Lombardy and Italy were elected and held their national assemblies, and at which all the princes of Italy attended. He spent a year in Italy on this occasion, returning to Germany in time to keep Easter 1056 at Paderborn. This year he held his interview with the King of France at Yvoi, in the Luxemburg country, in which the possession of Lorraine was so fiercely disputed that Henry III. offered to decide the right by single combat between the two principals. Henry of France did not expect so lively a retort and fled away by night.

Characteristics of the English, German, and French Nations. — This was almost the last important event of his life, and it exemplifies what more than once has been alluded to, the prowess of the German princes as distinguished from the reserve, if we call it no worse name, the cautious self-preservation so carefully maintained by the French. It is by no means a singular case that the French prince saves himself by cunning or flight where he ought to fight. Especially this is the case with Lewis VII., of whom, as the rival of our Henry II., so much is known. He possessed some good points, although not enough to give him the title of a good king; and almost the same may be said of his son, Philip Augustus. To find a German or an English king at this era who would have failed his knightly word in such a matter as Lewis did, or have absconded from the prospect of a fair struggle, would be quite impossible. It is an indication how far more the chivalrous spirit is German or Teutonic rather than French; and that the people who were ruled by such kings had not yet earned the name of a brave nation. The English kings and the German, as in the time of Tacitus, kept their hold on the popular imagination by a character for deeds of arms, and were still the leaders of their armies and ποιμένες λαῶν.

IMPORTANT DATES

Conrad II. (the Salic), 1024–1039.
Coronation in Milan, 1026.
Coronation at Rome, 1027.
Ernest of Bavaria fails to raise a rebellion, 1030.
Poland makes peace, 1031.
Conrad crowned King of Burgundy, 1033.
Expedition to Italy, 1037–1038.
Edict that holders of fiefs should not lose their lands except by the judgment of their peers, 1037.
Accession of Henry III., 1039.

CHAPTER IX

Henry III. and Otto III. compared.—Henry III. as-
cended the German throne at twenty-two, the age at
which Otto III. had died ; and the result of his policy,
so long as he survived to direct it, was very much what
the result of Otto's would have been if he had lived.   It
must be added, that the state of things which followed
his death could, considering the inveterate corruption
of the Roman court, have hardly been other than it
was.   If the brilliant impulsive genius of Otto could
have been substituted for the steady, single-eyed steers-
manship of Henry during the years in question, Otto
might have grown into a man like Henry as he gained
more experience of the world; but there is no proof
that Henry ever showed the qualities that give such
splendour to the youth and early manhood of Otto.
That Henry had the wise guidance of such a father
as Conrad the Salic, whilst Otto, although fairly well
cared for, enjoyed no such training, might have made
a great difference for after years.   The minority of
Otto might perhaps be compared with that of Henry
IV. ; the parallel is superficially the more obvious one.

But the conclusion must be that, had Otto lived, he could not have ruled better or done better for his kingdom, or exalted the imperial dignity more beneficially or more efficaciously, than Henry III. Both princes spent the early years of their reigns in Germany, and devoted the later ones to Italy ; both had a corrupt state of things in Rome to contend against, under which the one sank, the other was victorious ; both had a strong determined purpose of righteousness in his conduct toward the papal see; both were the strongest, most brilliant monarchs of their own time. But the power of Henry was to that of Otto as the substance to the shadow, as the full fruition to the early promise ; and yet the reign of his unhappy son was enough to destroy all that he had won, to degrade all that he had exalted. The reign of Henry III. is then a cardinal point in imperial and ecclesiastical history.

The Influence of Hildebrand.—Up to this moment, in the struggle between Germany and Italy, between the Empire and the Papacy, all the moral and personal weight had been on the German and imperial side. The Popes had no moral standing ground against Otto I. or Otto III., or against Henry II., Conrad the Salic, or Henry III. But from the death of Henry III. the direction of the papal court came into new hands ; Hildebrand infuses a new force and a purer spirit, and one that, under a king like Henry or Otto, might have reconciled even the two rival majesties of Pope and Emperor. But it was met in Henry IV. by a resistance in which the former character of imperial interference was lost ; the virtues and righteousnesses seemed to have changed sides, and notwithstanding a long contest and many faults and mistakes on both sides, the balance ultimately inclined to the reforma-

tion and exaltation of the Papacy; for such was the
result of the century of Franconian empire. But the
view of these things must go very much into the background in our examination of the condition of Germany
during these reigns; and there will be more to say
about rival houses and conflicting interests at home
than about the world-filling struggle between the regale
and the Pontificate.

The Position held by Henry III. in Europe.—Henry III.
was the strongest prince in Europe, and he was the
strongest prince that Europe had seen since Charles
the Great, in some respects stronger than Charles,
for, although his empire was smaller, its strength
was more concentrated and usable, and it was the
strength of a united and civilised nation as compared
with that of a divided and half barbarian one. He
was stronger than his father, as he was stronger
than Otto III. or Otto I. The empire reached its
nearest approach to the just ideal of imperialism, the
government by the wisest mind embodied in the most
righteous man. It is of course not to be concluded
that such imperialism is a good sort of government,
but there are ages and countries for which it is the
only form that is not distinctly bad ; and although, if
Germany had stood alone, it might at this time have
been more safely governed on freer or more elastic
methods, it would be unfair to judge it, surrounded as
it was by other hostile influences, as if such had been
the case. There is no proof that Henry III. founded
his power on wrong, or that he used it except in a
just and honest way.

Criticism of Hallam.—Hallam, with whom it is often
a pleasure to disagree, arguing on the sacred, eternal,
and unalterable principles of pure Whiggery, has laid

down, *ex cathedra*, that the ambitious measures of Henry III. prepared fifty years of calamity for his son ; and that it is easy to perceive that the misfortunes of Henry IV. were primarily occasioned by the jealousy with which repeated violations of their constitutional usages had inspired the nobility. Now this statement is so entirely opposed to the voice of history and popular belief and common sense, that it can be accounted for only on the supposition of invincible ignorance or invincible prejudice. The authority he gives is a quotation from Lambert of Hersfeld, stating that in the first year of Henry IV., the nobles of Saxony conspired to depose him out of revenge for the injuries they had received from his father ; and the bill of indictment against him includes the charges : (1) That Henry III. had retained after his accession to the throne, the fiefs that he had been invested with before. (2) That he heaped fiefs upon his own family as they became vacant. (3) That he deposed dukes without the consent of the diet. (4) That he put an end to the form of popular concurrence which had been usual when the investiture of a duchy was conferred.

Hallam's First Charge.—It is necessary to remark on these charges. With regard to (1), it may be stated that there was no constitutional right to make a German king resign his own fief when he came to the crown ; or if there were any such tradition, it had not been regularly acted upon. Hallam adduces the cases of Otto the Great, who, he says, resigned the duchy of Saxony, and Henry II. who resigned that of Bavaria ; a better instance would have been that of Conrad I., who resigned Franconia to his brother Eberhard. But (1) Henry the Fowler did not resign Saxony when he became king; and (2) Otto I. did not resign Saxony until the year 951, or later when he made Hermann Billung duke, nor did he put Hermann Billung in the place which himself and his father had occupied, but restricted his functions to those of guarding the marches of the Slavs, and so left the nobles of Saxony in a freer position and closer relation to the empire itself than they had before possessed. Otto II. was crowned king in his father's life, and Otto III. was a baby when he came to the crown; they had therefore nothing to resign; Henry II. certainly resigned Bavaria. Conrad the Salic had nothing to resign; Henry III. when he came to the throne held Alemannia and Bavaria by his father's gift. Alemannia he retained for six years, and Bavaria possibly for a short time, but this is uncertain. All that he did was to do as Otto I. had done with the largest, with the smallest of the duchies of Germany. There is evidence here that there was no such constitutional custom as Hallam supposes, and that if there was, Henry did not break it in any offensive degree; for unquestionably the nobles of the duchies would have more power, freedom of action, and direct access to the royal ear, continuing to be immediately subject to him, than when the authority of a duke was interposed. But if Henry had attempted a change, with the example of France before him he would have been amply justified. He certainly extinguished the duchy of Rhenish Franconia; but he placed the Count Palatine in the position formerly occupied by the Franconian dukes; and the creation of the Bishop of Bamberg had already reduced the duchy to be little more than the county of Worms: the title of Duke of the East Franks was borne by the bishops of Würzburg.

The Second Charge.—But (2) with regard to the second charge it is true that he heaped fiefs on his own family as fast as they became vacant : he gave Bavaria to his wife the Empress Agnes; afterwards he gave Bavaria to his two infant sons Henry IV. and Conrad as he had himself received it as a provision from his father, but Agnes was invested with it after his death in a great diet held at Ratisbon at Christmas 1056. It is not improbable that it may have been a point of honour for the emperor when he received the imperial crown, to divest himself of his duchies, but if that were the rule it was observed both by Otto I. and Henry III. and so far then Hallam's charges fall to the ground.

The Third and Fourth Charges.—The (3) third of the charges that he deposed, and (4) the fourth that he appointed, dukes without consent of the diet is not confirmed by any proofs; it is not likely to have been the case exactly, but the assertion is probably founded on the silence of the historians in relating the depositions and appointments. Hermannus Contractus says that he deposed Conrad Duke of Bavaria by the advice *quorundam principum.* It would be easy to go through the lists of the changes, but to do so would prove nothing; at all events would prove nothing of an innovating or aggressive policy such as Hallam attributes to this king.

The Importance of Correcting Hallam's Statements.— I have dwelt thus long upon this view of Hallam's because I am sure if it is true, my whole conception of the history of Germany is a mistake. But I am sure that Hallam has been misled by an *ex parte* view of some of his German authorities; and that the influences which I have already pointed out are quite

enough to account for the events of the next reign ;—
the antagonism of the northern and southern German
races, the rivalry between the German and Roman
churches, and the enmity between the empire and
the Papacy. If to these is added a long minority, a
bad education, an ungoverned disposition, domestic
difficulties and the rebellion of his own children, it
will be seen that there was every element and every
opening for discord, without intruding the principles
of 1688 to the disparagement of one of the greatest
and best of kings.

Henry III.'s Wars.—The war with Bohemia was
the one which occupied Henry chiefly in his earlier
years ; it ended in 1041 in the complete humiliation
of the Czechs who consented to pay tribute of 1500
marks. This was succeeded by a Hungarian war
which lasted until 1044, and ended in the restoration
of the deposed king Peter by Henry, and his investiture by the gift of a gilded lance, he and the
Hungarian nobles accepting the position of vassals.
In 1042, 1048, and 1052, he made excursions into
Burgundy, on each occasion having little trouble in
enforcing his authority. The death of Duke Gothelo
of Lorraine in 1044 produced a quarrel about the
succession between his two sons, which ended in
the establishment of Gerard of Alsace as hereditary
duke of Upper Lorraine, and a long series of struggles
for Lower Lorraine which do not end in this reign.
Perhaps the chief point of interest in this matter is
the fact that in this struggle, Duke Godfrey in alliance
with Count Baldwin of Flanders rebelled against
Henry. Baldwin went so far as to burn the imperial
palace at Nimwegen. It was in consequence of this
insult that Henry demanded the alliance and assist-

ance of Edward the Confessor, King of England, and he in compliance with the request buckled on his armour and betook himself to his fleet. The struggle ended as might be expected in the humiliation of the allies.

The Later Years of Henry's Reign—His Death, 1056.— Soon after this Henry devoted his attention to Italy more exclusively, and began to lose the affections of his more powerful subjects.[1] By way of strengthening his position after he became emperor, he bestowed, as has been already stated, the duchy of Alemannia, which he had held since his accession, on Otto the Count Palatine ; and gave the duchy of Carinthia, which had been held with Franconia, to Count Welf of Altorf in Swabia, thereby enormously increasing the power of that nobleman, whose family, originally Swabian, had given a wife to Louis the Pious and united now the character of indigenous princes with that of imperial lieutenants. From the marriage of Cunigunda the daughter of this Welf with Azzo of Este sprang the later Welfs of Bavaria, Saxony, Lüneburg, Brunswick, Hanover, and England. Henry was so long without issue after his second marriage that, on his illness as early as 1045, the Germans began to speculate on a succession, and fixed then on Henry Count Palatine—the monk, or the madman, as he was called. Henry however recovered and, on the birth of his son Henry in 1050, took measures for having him recognised as his successor; this was done at Goslar at Christmas 1051. In 1053 the succession was assured to him by his election as king at Tribur ; and in 1054 he was crowned king at Aix-la-Chapelle by the Archbishop of Cologne.

---

[1] In 1046 Henry was crowned emperor by Clement II. ; in 1048 Henry nominated the Bishop of Toul as Pope Leo IX.

The last year of Henry's life, according to Hermann Contractus, was marked by much discontent; he says that "murmuring more and more against the emperor, they complained that he was gradually declining from the way in which he had begun to walk, and ought to have advanced daily, *i.e.* from the way of righteousness, peace, piety and the fear of God and love of virtue, into habits of covetousness and carelessness, and falling much away from his former self." Of course this may have been the case; the possession of almost unlimited power is the most trying of all things to a man. It may also be that the charges were false and that their very vagueness proves them to have slight foundation. But it is pretty certain (1) that any devotion showed to the Imperial as opposed to German interests would be interpreted as ambition and negligence, and that the later years of Henry were largely so devoted to Italian politics; and (2) that his health was declining long before his death. His father had lived to be fifty; he himself only reached thirty-nine. He was hunting at Bothfeld on the border of Saxony and Thuringia, when he received the news of the complete defeat of his forces, his Saxon forces, by the barbarians on the Lusatian frontier. Had he been in ordinary health, the news would have roused him to fresh exertion, but, acting upon a morbid temperament and decayed health, it was fatal. He gradually declined, and just had time to get the succession of his son confirmed by the Pope, the princes, and bishops, before his death. The Pope Victor II., Gebhard of Eichstadt, was with him at the last moment.

The Accession of Henry IV., 1056.—The reign of Henry IV. now opens upon us. A child of six years old

who may be compared with Otto III., Henry was under
the guardianship of his mother Agnes of Aquitaine.
His was a most unhappy reign, almost unparalleled in
the annals of Europe for its length of wretchedness.
It will be well to divide it into three divisions, if only for
the sake of clearness :—the minority and youth of
Henry ; his struggles after his majority ; his final decline.
The first period shall extend from 1056 to 1073, a period
which is marked by the beginning of the quarrels with
the Pope and the Saxon wars ; from 1073 to 1092 when
he raised his eldest son to the throne will be the second ;
and from 1092 to 1106 when he died in the extremity of
degradation, and it is to be hoped in penitence, will be
the third.[1]

Henry IV.'s Character.—The character of Henry IV. is
very variously read, the violent Romanist of course
condemns him utterly and the violent Protestant as
gratuitously acquits him.   But the contemporaneous
accounts, however one sided they may seem, will
present a character possessed of some bright and many
endearing qualities, entirely debased by self-indulgence
and unrestrained passion, in which education has rather
produced an evil than attempted a good effect.   Bad
education and a violent temperament, passions encouraged by his guardians, pandered to by his companions, unchecked by any lasting religious feeling—
these are the colours in which his youth is painted.
Out of such a youth, unless by the discipline of grinding
adversity, a good manhood cannot spring ; the best that
can be expected is a penitent old age, for adversity in
manhood is an unpractical discipline for kings.   There
he stands, however, an abandoned youth ; who has a

---

[1] Lambert of Hersfeld is well worth careful study, and a full account of
Henry's reign will he found in Milman's " History of Latin Christianity."

brilliant, melancholy but unrepented manhood, and a premature and degraded old age. If his sins were great, few men have borne heavier punishment than Henry IV.

First Period of the Reign, 1056–1073—*The Growth of Antagonism between the Empire and Papacy.*—Almost directly after the death of Henry III., the discontent of the Saxon nobles broke out into rebellion, headed by Otto, a candidate for one of the margraviates into which under the Billung administration the old duchy of Saxony had been broken up. But the rebellion, although formidable, soon came to an end, Otto being slain in single combat in June 1057 by Bruno Count of Brunswick. The next month, Pope Victor II. died, and with that event the harmony which had subsisted between the empire and the Papacy in consequence of the prudent policy of Henry III. was dissolved, and for the rest of the reign the history of Germany is inextricably interwoven with the politics of Italy. Pope Victor had been the intimate friend of Henry and Agnes, and, for the short time he survived the former, had exercised the whole power of Pope and emperor. But upon his death the first sign of the terrible breach that was to come, became visible. Frederick of Lorraine, the brother of Duke Godfrey the husband of the Marchioness Beatrice, and Henry's great enemy in both Germany and Italy, was elected Pope. He was a good austere man acting on the principles of Hildebrand, of reformation at Rome and independence of the emperor; he reigned little more than six months, and then after a disputed election, Nicholas II. was placed in the papal chair by the influence of Hildebrand, who united in his favour both the empress and Duke Godfrey. The policy of Nicholas decided the

remaining history of the century. His two great acts
were: (1) the law by which the regulated the election of
future popes, confining it to the cardinals, to the exclusion both of the people and of the emperor; and (2)
the alliance with the Normans, by which he hoped to
raise a counterpoise to the German influence in Italy.
He died in 1061. From 1061 to 1073 Alexander II.
reigned, in spite of the opposition of Cadalous Bishop
of Parma, who stood forth as the nominee of Guibert
the chancellor, the rival politician to Hildebrand, and
as the protector of the abuses which Hildebrand had
made it his mission to correct:—simony and clerical
marriages.

Triumph of the Hildebrandine Party, 1065.—During
these years the fortunes of Henry IV. were gradually declining. His mother Agnes, who of course held the
policy of her husband, would naturally have acted in
opposition to the schemes of Hildebrand and Nicholas
II., but the German bishops for the time, and a body
of the princes under the influence of Duke Godfrey,
were apparently in alliance with the Hildebrandine
party, probably united only by common jealousy of
the imperial influence. In this interest it was that
Henry was withdrawn in the year 1061 from his
mother's side, kidnapped in fact by Hanno Archbishop
of Cologne and Otto Count of Nordheim, the leader of
the Saxon party, in whose favour Agnes had that very
year divested herself of the duchy of Bavaria. The
bishops thus mismanaged the affairs of the empire for
some years in Henry's name, their power being partly
counterbalanced by the influence of the empress and
her court. As Henry grew older, he threw himself
into the hands of Adalbert Bishop of Bremen, who did
him not less mischief by indulgence than Hanno had

done by strictness; between the two rival prelates he
was entirely misled and disqualified from ever becoming
a good king. The policy of Hanno favoured the papal
party, that of Adalbert the antipapal, namely that of
Cadalous, who in 1063 was emboldened to take up his
position in Rome itself. But the party of Hanno made
a vigorous effort to overthrow Adalbert and regain their
influence over Henry; in this they succeeded at Christmas 1065. Alexander II. was henceforth triumphant,
and the policy of Hildebrand acquiesced in until his
death. But North Italy was at war on this account
during Henry's whole reign, and Germany was too much
weakened by internal divisions to interfere with effect.

Henry IV. rapidly loses his Influence.—Henry's influence was in fact quickly becoming of no account.
As he advanced to manhood his dissipated habits
became very notorious, and Germany had never yet
had a king who defied all laws of morality. He detested
his wife and was only prevented by the papal interference from being divorced from her by the German
bishops whom he had bribed. He offended the Saxons
by the exclusive appointment of South German officials,
and suppressed with great difficulty the revolt of Dedo
margrave of Lausitz at the head of the Thuringian
nobles; while Otto of Nordheim who, although a
Saxon, had been made by Agnes duke of Bavaria,
was deprived of his duchy in 1071, and having a real
grievance put himself at the head of the Saxons.
Such then was the condition of Germany until 1073,
when Henry saw his influence at the lowest point.
He himself was a man with vicious tastes, to whom
the bishops were ready to pander in every way if only
they could maintain their own political influence at
the expense of his. Moreover his dukes and counts were

quarrelling over the limits of their estates and deciding their quarrels or aggravating them by private war.

Growth of the Papal Influence.—All this time the Papacy was daily purifying and strengthening itself under the wholesome tonic of Hildebrandine policy, while the empire was daily being weakened and degraded. As might be expected the good sense of men and nations was placing them on the side of reformation, now represented in the Papacy as before it had been represented by the emperor. Saxony the strongest and most thoroughly German of the German nations, partly by provincial jealousy and partly by actual neglect, was being driven away from the emperor towards the Papacy, and with the papal party henceforth Saxony is closely bound up and will continue so until the end of the Middle Ages.

Second Period of Henry's Reign, 1073–1106.—The second division of the reign of Henry IV. begins in 1073. This period brings out the good points, the brilliant abilities of Henry, and gives us reason to admire the efforts he made to cast off the influence of his early vice and indolence. On the death of Alexander II. in 1073 Hildebrand himself took the Papacy as Gregory VII., and did so with the consent of the emperor, which he condescended to ask for with the significant hint that it would be his best policy to decline. But although Henry must have been aware, from his knowledge of Gregory's previous policy, that a collision would come unless he himself were prepared to give way to the supremacy of the spiritual power, an actual breach did not occur until 1075 when Gregory, by the publication of his law against lay investitures, threatened the extinction of nearly all that was left of the imperial power.

The Saxon Revolt, 1073–1075.—Henry's difficulties in Germany began almost from the day of Gregory's election. The day after that election the Saxons met at Goslar and were provoked by Henry's insolence to declare war. The misgivings which they had of him before, were increased by the fact that he had built a series of mountain castles to keep them in order; and had even, as they supposed or alleged, entered into a league with the Danes, to reduce them to slavery. They insist that the castles shall be destroyed; that he shall dismiss his favourites (chiefly Swabians), and rule with the advice of his princes. The principal rebels were bishops, of whom the chief was the Archbishop of Magdeburg, but Otto of Nordheim, the dispossessed Duke of Bavaria, whom the Saxons wished to elect as their king, was the leading spirit. Magnus Billung, the heir of the duchy, was kept out of his succession by Henry; he threw in his lot with Otto of Nordheim; Welf the new Duke of Bavaria, and Rudolf Duke of Swabia, brother-in-law of Henry, and Berthold Duke of Carinthia, seeing that Henry was as devoid of counsel as of moral strength, withdrew from him; and he was reduced to go round to the principal nobles as a petitioner, entreating their aid against the Saxons. For two years he endeavoured by promises and petitions to disarm them or to divide them. They, on the other hand, contemplated the election of a new king; the Archbishop of Mainz was ready to crown Rudolf of Swabia, who although still adhering to Henry, was marked out as his rival for the empire. The Archbishop of Cologne even thought of calling in William the Bastard, the now triumphant conqueror and ruler of England. When Henry was reduced to the lowest estate, only the faithful city of Worms being left to him, his fortunes took a sudden change ; the wavering princes returned to their allegiance ; the army was placed under the command of Rudolf, and in the battle of Hohenburg, June 12, 1075, Henry was completely victorious. He used his triumph very ruthlessly. Otto of Nordheim, the Archbishop of Magdeburg, and others being imprisoned. Thus he lost the opportunity of conciliating the Saxons. At Christmas, however, he persuaded the princes collected at Goslar to accept his infant son Conrad as his successor and their king.

Beginning of the Investiture Contest, 1075.—The scene now changes and the Pope comes into the foreground. Gregory VII. during Henry's extremity had endeavoured to make hard terms with him ; the victory of Hohenburg elated his enemies. In reliance on the German party Cencius made his famous seizure of Gregory (Dec. 25, 1075). The Pope escaped through the enthusiasm of the populace ; and immediately wrote to Henry to insist on the surrender of the investitures, summoning him to Rome to defend himself on the 22nd of February 1076. Henry in defence called his diet at Worms for January 24, 1076, and declared the Pope deposed. Gregory received the news in the Lateran council, to which he had summoned Henry ; he excommunicated the king and the prelates who had joined in the sentence and declared Henry deposed from the kingdom. Henry received the news at Utrecht, on March 27, and the Bishop of Utrecht excommunicated Gregory. A new conspiracy among the German princes followed, this time composed of the men who had stood on Henry's side, Rudolf of Swabia, Welf of Bavaria, and Berthold of Carinthia. Henry thereupon released his Saxon prisoners in the hope of setting them against his new enemies but they joined them; his arms were unsuccessful, the Pope was relentless, and Henry's bishops lost their courage and bought reconciliation by submission. The confederates (nobles and bishops) met at Tribur on October 27, and determined to elect a new king if Henry would not submit. Seeing himself utterly helpless, he submitted; the Pope should come and hold a diet at Augsburg on February 2, 1077, in the meantime he would dismiss his court and forces and live as a private man.

Canossa, January, 1077.—Henry made use, however, of the interval to make that sad and ever memorable pilgrimage to Canossa in January 1077, where by the most abject humiliation he obtained from the Pope a formal absolution and restoration to communion which the Pope tried to make an appeal to the judgment of God. From this degradation Henry seemed to acquire strength, his old friends rallied to him and even the Germans generally felt that the Pope had gone too far. Gregory dreaded to visit Germany, and fearing an attack from Henry, fled from Mantua, where he was preparing to hold his council, back to Canossa.

Diet at Forcheim, March 1077—*Civil War,* 1077–1080. —In March 1077 the German princes met at Forcheim and elected Rudolf of Swabia king. He swore to leave the election of bishops free and not to attempt to make the empire hereditary. The Pope was to be propitiated by the first promise, the princes by the second; he was consecrated by the Archbishop of Mainz on March 26th and the Pope sent him a crown. Civil war now began. Henry returned to Germany; his party gained new strength; the Pope hardly even tried to support

Rudolf. At last on March 7, 1080, he summoned courage to proceed to a second excommunication and deposition and actually acknowledged the rival king. Henry's reply was to depose Gregory and elect a new Pope. This was done at Brixen, June 25, 1080, and the new Pope was Guibert of Ravenna. Three months after, the decisive victory of the Elster was won. Rudolf was killed by Godfrey of Bouillon and the king was again supreme.

War between Henry and Gregory, 1081–1084—*Death of Gregory*, 1085.—Henry now descended into Italy and besieged the Pope in Rome. For three years the siege lasted, Italy and Germany remaining attent on the issue. The Norman allies of Gregory made no sign. By Christmas 1083, Henry was master of all Rome except the Castle of S. Angelo; Guibert was crowned Pope in March 1084, and from him Henry received the imperial crown on Easter day, March 31, 1084. Almost immediately after he was compelled to retire before the Normans who very nearly destroyed Rome in the excess of their triumph. Under the protection of these terrible allies Gregory retired, still breathing excommunications, into the South of Italy and then at Salerno the following May 1085 he died.

War in Germany, 1084–1092.—Neither the defeat on the Elster, nor the later successes of Henry in Italy had, however, subdued the spirit of the Germans. Hermann of Luxemburg was chosen king by the Swabians at Eisleben in Thuringia. Otto of Nordheim was still the moving spirit of opposition among the lay princes, but Otto died in 1083 ; and, on the return of Henry from Italy in 1084, the war in Saxony revived and Germany saw two kings, as Italy had seen two

Popes, fulminating spiritual and temporal threats against one another. Notwithstanding occasional successes and the pertinacious support of the successors of Gregory, Hermann's star declined; in 1087 the young Conrad was crowned at Aix-la-Chapelle; and in 1088 the Saxons deserted their king Hermann and he retired into Lorraine, laid aside his title and soon after died. With the final submission of the Saxons in 1092, the second period of the reign ends.

Third Period of the Reign, 1092–1106.—Already however the miseries of the third and most wretched period were beginning;—the corruption, by the Countess Matilda, of the young Conrad; his desertion of his father, the unrelenting hatred of Pope Urban II. (the equally persistent, and more cunning successor of Hildebrand); that frightful council of Piacenza in 1095 where Henry was so cruelly humbled and belied by his wife; the desertion of Henry that followed the sentence against him; the league between his undutiful son and the Welfs, who, all powerful in Bavaria, were nearly as powerful in Italy through the marriage of the younger Welf with the Countess Matilda; the bestowal by Matilda of her estates upon the Church, and the consequent submission of Welf to Henry; the vicissitudes of the Antipope Guibert; the repudiation by Henry of his eldest son, and coronation of Henry the younger at Aix-la-Chapelle in 1099; the recovery of the imperial power in Germany; Henry's programme of repentance and pilgrimage; the rebellion of the younger Henry in 1104; his pretended submission and treacherous seizure of his father; the forced resignation, the flight to Cologne and Liege; the defeat and imprisonment of the father by the son; his literal destitution and even beggary, followed by his death on

August 7, 1106 at Liege :—all this is detailed for you
in the most dramatic way by Milman, with whose moral
consideration of the crisis it is difficult to entirely agree.
With regard to the internal condition of Germany the
history of these years contains little which is new after
the submission of Hermann of Luxemburg, and that
little as it affects the combinations of parties and the
aggrandisement of the rival houses, will be alluded to
in the account of the following reigns. Great part of
the interest of this period is personal and great part
is ecclesiastical, with which here we have less to do.
In spite of all the sins of Henry IV. we dislike his
enemies so much that we are inclined to pity him if
not to feel a stronger interest in his most unhappy
fortune.

DUKES

Bavaria.—Henry, 1025 ; Conrad, 1047–1053, deposed in diet ; Henry,
    1052, heir apparent, afterwards Henry IV.

Alemannia.—Conrad, 982–997 ; Hermann, 997–1004 ; Hermann, 1004–
    1012 ; Ernest I. of Babenberg, 1012–1015 ; Ernest II., 1015,
    son of the Empress Gisela by her first husband Ernest I., died
    1030 ; Hermann IV. and Conrad II., 1030–1039 ; Henry the
    Emperor, 1039–1045 ; Otto Count Palatine, 1045–1047 ; Otto III.
    of Schweinfurth, 1047–1057.

Saxony.—Bernard Billung, 1004–1062.

Franconia.—Conrad III., 1004–1011 ; Conrad IV., 1011–1039, the
    title extinguished.

Lorraine.—Gothelo died, 1044.

Upper Lorraine.—Gothelo II., 1043–1046 ; Albert of Alsace, 1046–
    1048 ; Gerard of Alsace, 1048–1070.

Lower Lorraine.—Godfrey the Bearded, 1044–1048 ; Frederick of
    Luxembourg, 1049–1065 ; Godfrey again, 1065–1069 ; Godfrey le
    Bossu, son, 1069 ; Godfrey le Barbu, married in 1055, Beatrice,
    daughter of Frederick of Upper Lorraine, 1026–1033, widow of
    Boniface, whose daughter Matilda married his son Godfrey le
    Bossu.

IMPORTANT DATES

War with Bohemia, 1041.
Disorder in Lorraine, 1044 *seq.*
War with Hungary, 1043–1044.
Leo IX. visits Germany, 1049.
Birth of Henry's son, 1050.
Henry makes the Bishop of Eichstadt Pope as Victor II., 1054.
Henry in Lombardy, 1055.
Henry's death, 1056.
Henry IV., 1056–1106.
Death of Pope Victor II., 1057.
Election of Pope Nicholas II., 1059.
Hanno seizes the Emperor, 1061.
Triumph of the Hildebrandine party, 1065.
Revolt of the Saxons, 1073–1075.
Beginning of the Investiture struggle, 1075.
Henry's submission at Canossa, 1077.
Civil War in Germany, 1077–1080.
Henry in Italy, 1081–1084.
Death of Gregory VII., 1085.
Submission of the Saxons, 1092.
The Council of Piacenza, 1095.
Rebellion of the younger Henry, 1104.

CHAPTER X

The Importance of the Reign of Henry V., 1106–1125.—
In this chapter will be shortly reviewed the character
of the three reigns that intervene between Henry IV.
and Frederick Barbarossa ; those of Henry V., Lothair
II., and Conrad III. The first of these, that of Henry
V., has much more importance given to it in general
history than the other two, being as it seems the
continuation of the struggle in which his father had
perished, between the papal and imperial powers, on
the subject of investitures. The importance of this
struggle had quite overshadowed the national history
of the time, and, whilst itself is abundantly illustrated,
has engrossed nearly all the illustrative power of both
contemporary and later historians. To us it would
be interesting rather in its bearings upon Germany
than on its own merits, but the marks that it has left
on German history, although broad, are not distinct.
An attempt will now be made (1) to estimate the character of Henry ; (2) to sketch his proceedings in the
matter of the Papacy, and (3) to enumerate the political

changes which took place in Germany either in consequence of, or in parallel sequence with those proceedings. It is necessary, first of all, to distinguish between the rebellion of Conrad the elder son of Henry IV., and that of Henry V.; and see the light thus thrown upon the character of the latter.

Conrad's Revolt against Henry IV.—Conrad's revolt against his father was a religious revolt. He was unquestionably a devotee of a marked stamp, and had fallen under the influence on the one hand of the Countess Matilda, an enthusiastic and unscrupulously pious Italian partisan, and on the other of his stepmother, Queen Praxedes, of whom the only thing that it can be said is, that, if she were not mad, she was the most hideously wicked woman in modern history. The story of her fabricated wrongs, credited perhaps all the more readily by a boy, whose knowledge of the realities of vice was less distinct than his hatred of the habits prevalent in his father's court, worked upon a morbid imagination, full of the superstitions of the time; and from a religious enthusiast he became a rebel forsaking, as he doubtless thought, father and home, for the sake of the kingdom of heaven. When he found that he had not the success ultimately that he had thought himself entitled to, he subsided into the insignificance for which he was much better fitted than for empire.

Character of the Emperor, Henry V.—But Henry V. was very different; with him the avenging of the Church's wrongs was but a pretext for the designs of his ruthless, unnatural ambition. He was not even persuaded by enthusiastic women, nor invited to the struggle by an unscrupulous pontiff. On his own head rests the guilt of a rebellion undertaken against a father who loved him with the tenderest affection, and who had long ceased to offend in the ways which had seemed to Conrad to justify his own conduct. Henry's whole life was one of cruel, unrelenting selfishness, which nothing could turn aside, no success could abate; he was a thorough tyrant who, but that the miseries of the late reign had cut the imperial wings, would have shown the world at large what he was. From the moment that his father's death put him in possession of the remains of imperial power, and whilst the guilty complicity of the German prelates and princes still united them with him, he took up the policy of his father with regard to the Papacy, and on the very point on which the disputes began, that of the lay investitures. He acquired the royal power by his father's resignation at Christmas 1105, and immunity for the time by his death in the following August. His whole career from that time was one of falsehood, injustice, and avarice. Two months after his accession, the Pope in the council of Guastalla renewed his condemnation of investiture by lay hands. Henry did not at once declare himself to have taken up the cause which his father had struggled for, but invited the Pope to Augsburg to settle the affairs of the Church. Pope Paschal did not venture to comply with the invitation, and Henry in consequence defied the papal law by proceeding to invest bishops as had been done before. The Pope went to France, but Henry would not be dealt with from that country, nor treat except upon his own ground.

Henry's Coronation at Rome, April 13, 1111.—Hostilities were, however, deferred, and Henry undertook to appear at Rome in a year; then he was to have the imperial crown and the question was to be settled.

It was not until January 1110 that Henry prepared for his journey; strengthened himself by the adhesion of a diet at Regensburg, and marched into Italy with the force and in the spirit of a despot. Burning and plundering an unresisting country he advanced through Lombardy, declaring the purpose of his visit to be— (1) the winning of the imperial crown; (2) the pacification of Lombardy; (3) the protection of the Church. Unopposed he reached Rome early in 1111, and, by the terrors of his name and character, compelled the Pope to make an agreement which was to be ratified on the day of the coronation. Throughout the Church the prelates were to resign the regalia, the emperor to give up the right of investiture. On the 12th of February Pope and king met in S. Peter's, and Henry was saluted as emperor, but neither trusted the other, neither would be the first to give up the point he contended for. The assembly broke up without a coronation, and the Pope and cardinals went away as prisoners. After two months' resistance Paschal, April 12, 1111, surrendered the right of investiture to Henry and the day after crowned him at S. Peter's.

Henry's Struggle with Paschal. — The tables were now turned on the Papacy and this humiliation set against the abasement of Henry IV. at Canossa. Amongst the other terms of submission, Paschal said that he would take no revenge, and Henry went away safe and triumphant. The clergy, however, were not satisfied, and it took little persuasion to make the Pope anxious to repudiate the agreement. In March 1112, after the immediate fear of the emperor was removed, the concession of Paschal was repudiated by a Lateran Council and the breach was completed by the excommunication of the emperor by the Council of Vienne

(Paschal not being present), in which the temporal claim to investitures was declared to be heresy. This was confirmed by another Lateran Council in 1116. This excommunication greatly weakened Henry's hold on Germany ; but his second visit to Italy was consequent on the death in 1115 of the Countess Matilda, who left all her estates to the see of Rome. This bequest, if it had taken effect, would have made Paschal supreme in Italy ; but the emperor immediately put in a claim for her fiefs as escheated, and for her allodial estates as secured to Duke Welf of Bavaria by her marriage settlement. He entered Italy in March 1116, took possession of the estates, and sent on his messengers to Rome. After some ineffectual discussions he marched on Rome, Paschal retiring before him ; there he spent Easter and retired northward in the autumn. Paschal died January 1118.

Struggles of Henry with Popes Gelasius and Calixtus II. —The Concordat of Worms, 1122.—His successor Gelasius refusing to ratify the act of April 1111, Henry refused to recognise him, and after several sacrilegious riots at Rome, forced the Archbishop of Braga on the see as antipope, under the name of Gregory VIII. Gelasius retired into France where he died, and was succeeded by Calixtus II. (Guy Archbishop of Vienne, who had excommunicated Henry in 1112). Calixtus was a vigorous man, and took bold measures. He came to Rome, and captured Sutri and the antipope in it. His legate at the same time appealed to the Saxons who rebelled and forced Henry to propose terms of agreement. So suddenly was the great quarrel brought to a conclusion. In February 1122, the peace of the Church, the Concordat of Worms, was settled. The emperor surrendered investiture by the ring and staff,

M

the Pope allowed that all elections of prelates should be made in the presence of the emperor or his deputies, and the German bishops shall receive their temporalities by the touch of the royal sceptre. So ends the great struggle. The leading points of its effect on Germany may be considered to be : (1) the maintenance of a basis of opposition to imperial despotism, of which any oppressed or offended prince, secular or clerical, could avail himself; (2) the creation of a series of petty wars throughout the country which extended through the reign and gave the emperor constant opportunities of injustice and tyranny ; (3) the weakening of the imperial power by these means more than it had ever been weakened by the disputes of Henry IV. The great feudatories made enormous strides towards independence under Henry V., which indeed were temporarily lost under Frederick Barbarossa, but which still illustrates the increasing weakness of the central principle.

Changes in the Duchies.—The changes which took place in the duchies and the conclusions which may be drawn from them will now be described, for it must not be forgotton that, after all, the ecclesiastical princes were larger gainers even than the secular ones. They gained on both hands, alternating between the empire and the Papacy, and drawing new temporal and new spiritual privileges by way of reward. But the growth of this power is a great feature of the reign of Henry IV. as well, and may be partly accounted for by the decline of the older houses of the great duchies, and by the constant bestowal of the fiefs on the younger members and officers of the imperial family, who with constantly diminishing territories and powers, had also a constantly diminishing hold on the affections of their subjects. As they decline the spiritual lordships rise. Of the five nations, Franconia has now subsided into a subordinate place. Henry III. had let it fall out of the list of duchies, but in 1116 Henry V. revived it in favour of his nephew Conrad of Hohenstaufen. A new dynasty had been founded in Bavaria in 1071 under the Welfs. Welf VI. succeeded about 1101 ; he was the husband of the Countess Matilda, and a faithful adherent of the emperor. His brother and successor, Henry the Black, by his marriage with the heiress of the Billung dukes of Saxony, laid the foundation of the power of the Welfs in North Germany. It should be stated that Welf VI. and Henry the Black were the children of Welf V. by Judith of Flanders, the widow of Tostig, Earl of Northumbria, son of Godwin and brother of our Harold. The duchy of Saxony, as has been said, hardly less than that of Franconia, was being gradually dismembered ; still in name it continued to subsist. Duke Magnus Billung, whose imprisonment had been the cause of the Saxon war of 1073, died in 1106; and the male line of that ancient house was extinct.[1] The allodial estates, *i.e.* Lüneburg, fell to Henry the Black of Bavaria with Wulfhild the heiress ; the fief was bestowed on Lothair, emperor and count of Supplinburg, who had married Richenza, the grand-daughter and heiress of Otto of Nordheim, daughter of Henry the Fat, and gained with her the allods of the old house of Brunswick, which she inherited from her mother Gertrude. Lothair thus got both the Billung fiefs and the Nordheim and Bruns-

---

[1] Magnus Billung had two daughters, one, Wulfhild, married Henry the Black, Duke of Bavaria and Saxony, and Prince of Sardinia ; the other, Elicke, married Otto of Ballenstadt, Count of Ascania ; she had Soltwedel and Brandenburg.

wick allods; his daughter carried the inheritance to Henry the Proud (Duke of Saxony and Bavaria, died 1139), son of Henry the Black, who had the Billung allods, and under whom and his son Henry the Lion the old duchy of Saxony was ultimately reconstituted. Lothair (the emperor 1125–1137) thus became Duke of Saxony.

Swabia and Lorraine under Henry IV. and V.—Swabia, after the death of Rudolf in the battle of the Elster, was given by Henry IV. to his brother-in-law Frederick I. of Hohenstaufen : his son Frederick succeeded him in 1105 : he also was a faithful friend of his uncle the emperor, and fought his most important battles for him. Lorraine was, as it had been under Henry IV., the part where the imperial influence was weakest, and the ecclesiastical domination consequently the strongest. But at the time of Henry's accession the duchy of Lower Lorraine was held by Henry of Limbourg, the one faithful friend of his father ; the reward of the fidelity was his deprivation by the new king. He was succeeded by his brother Godfrey, who after a short struggle remained in possession.

Henry V.'s Visits to Italy, and his German Wars, 1111–1116. — It has been already stated that in Henry's earlier years he had at least the secular princes, who had joined against his father, on his side, as well as the ecclesiastical ones who recognised the papal excommunication. He was himself to taste the same cup, though not so bitterly, which his father had drunk. Until 1111 he was employed, however, only in border warfare ; in 1107 he had to reduce Count Robert of Flanders ; and to restore a banished duke to Bohemia ; and in 1109 to compel the payment of tribute by the Hungarians and Poles by force of arms. It was not

until this was done that he was able to make his first
expedition into Italy ; at that time he was all powerful.
The excommunication by the Council of Vienne in 1112
broke up the unity of his power ; and on the great
occasion of his marriage with Matilda, daughter of
Henry I. of Normandy, at Mainz in 1114, a conspiracy
was formed against him, in which every prince of
Germany, except his nephews Frederick and Conrad
of Hohenstaufen and the Count Palatine Godfrey,
joined. Henry left the management of the war to his
nephew Frederick, who was very successful against the
insurgents. His proceedings are briefly sketched by
Otto of Freising, who is now becoming the contemporary historian, but not with sufficient distinctness
to enable us to ascertain details except so far as his
victory over the Archbishop of Mainz is concerned.
Saxony, however, was continuously the seat of war.
Lothair, the duke of his own nomination,[1] joined against
him, even before the Italian expedition, and was for
some time disgraced. The rebellion which broke out
there after the excommunication of Vienne was cruelly
put down, and it was probably in revenge for this
treatment that Lothair joined his people in the revolt
of 1114. He even inflicted a severe defeat on Henry
at Welpesholtz in the county of Mansfeld Feb. 11, 1115.
This Saxon War was not quite appeased until 1126
when all the rebels were reconciled at Goslar. The
only other important war was that by which the Count
of Bar was compelled to perform his feudal obligations
and to surrender the county of Verdun, 1113, 1123, 1124.

Henry's French War and Death, 1125.—In his last year

---

[1] Lothair of Supplinburg had acquired the Saxon duchy through his marriage
with Richenza, niece of Egbert of Meissen and grand-daughter of Otto of
Nordheim.

Henry V. felt himself free for foreign war ; and undertook to attack Louis VI. of France, partly as an enemy
of his father-in-law the King of England, partly as an
ally of the Pope. But he only got as far as Metz on
his way to Rheims, and then turned back; his army,
we conclude from the Saxon annalist, who relates that
the Germans dislike war on foreign nations, declined
to follow him. The last that is heard of him is in
Lower Lorraine where he was taking measures to allay
the discontent of his nobles. He had, as the story
goes, formed an idea, derived originally from his father-
in-law, of reducing the whole of his dominions to pay
a general tax, on the principle under which the Domes-
day Book of England had been drawn up. On this
journey he came to Utrecht, where during Pentecost
he died on May 23, of a sudden attack of constitutional
disease. He left no heir but commended the empire
to his wife Matilda, and consigned the jewels of the
imperial crown to her, to be kept in the castle of Trifels
until a new election should be made. She, it is said,
sent them to England to her father. Henry was buried
at Speyer beside his father, whom he had scarcely, after
many years, obtained leave from the Pope to bury at
all. But popular belief would not be contented that
such a son should die without having his reward in this
world. According to the story, one night, whilst at
Utrecht in his palace, he disappeared from the eyes
of men. The empress had gone to bed and left him
in his hall or presence chamber, and waited for him,
but he never came nor was ever seen by any who
recognised him. Some believed that he fled to England
and there lived as a hermit somewhere near Chester,
where Harold also was believed to be living ; others
said that he was at Solothurn in Burgundy. From

Solothurn in 1138, came forth a pretender declaring that he was the emperor, but Lothair got hold of him and made him a monk at Cluny; a proceeding which may be interpreted to show either that he was above or that he was below severer punishment.

Election of Lothair of Supplinburg as Emperor (Lothair II.), 1125.—In Henry the great house of Franconia ended, having in the last two reigns worn out the affection and patience of the Germans. A strong re-action in favour of the Saxon and Roman parties was naturally to be expected and it came. Of the form of proceedings which followed the vacancy of the empire an exact narration has been preserved. The Arch-bishop of Mainz summoned the princes of Germany to meet at Mainz on the Feast of S. Bartholomew; the summons was obeyed with such hearty goodwill that not less than 60,000 fighting men assembled. The Saxons and Bavarians occupied one side of the river, the Swabians and Burgundians the other. On the appointed day the princes met and chose out of their number, that is out of the princes of Bavaria, Swabia, Franconia, and Saxony, ten as a committee, by whose choice the whole body would be determined. The ten chose three as the most worthy to sit on the throne of Otto—Frederick of Hohenstaufen, Duke of Swabia, the nephew of the late emperor, Leopold, Margrave of Austria, who had married Agnes the sister of Henry after the death of the first Frederick of Hohenstaufen, and Lothair, Duke of Saxony. The Duke of Swabia was clearly the natural successor to his uncle, both by birth and by desert; and the other two nominees refused the honour. But on Duke Frederick presenting himself to the assembly for elec-tion, Albert, Archbishop of Mainz, the determined enemy of Henry V. and all his policies, rose and asked whether the three nominees would agree without opposition to accept the determination of the diet. Lothair and Leopold promised; Frederick refused to do so without taking counsel of his friends; and this hesitation induced the diet unanimously to reject him. The following day Lothair was elected by acclamation, under the influence of the archbishop. The nobles of Bavaria and Swabia were reluctant to accept such a tumultuary decision, but the persuasions of the papal legate prevailed; Lothair was formally elected and received the homage of his rival Duke Frederick. He was crowned at Aix-la-Chapelle on the 13th of September.

The Reign of Lothair.—Lothair reigned rather more than twelve years, retaining until the last year the duchy of Saxony in his own hands. During the whole of this time he showed himself a faithful son of the Church and a faithful patron of the Saxons, the two influences that placed him on the throne. He even went so far as to suffer the clergy to withhold their homage for the fiefs they held of the empire; nor did he show any great alacrity in demanding the imperial crown which had so embittered the relations between his predecessors and the Popes. His first five years were spent in Germany, where he had his work set to obtain practical recognition from his late competitors. After a campaign in the chronic war between the Saxons and Bohemians, in which Lothair was successful, he undertook the difficult task of reducing the Dukes of Swabia and Franconia to the level of the other princes. He besieged Nürnberg but retired before the two brothers; he also seized Speyer which they had garrisoned; but, although assisted by the Archbishop of Mainz and the Duke of Bavaria, he was obliged to retire from it. On this

successful resistance Conrad, the younger Hohenstaufen
brother, was elected anti-king by his adherents, and in
1123 crossed into Lombardy where he was crowned
at Monza. The German archbishops excommunicated
him, and this sentence was confirmed by the Pope
Honorius II. The struggle lasted for four or five years
longer, but was confined to that part of Germany
which was under the rule of Frederick of Swabia.
Lothair's general was his son-in-law, Henry the Proud,
Duke of Bavaria, who, although frequently discomfited
by Frederick when they met in person, was generally victorious in his absence and gained upon him gradually.
Nürnberg surrendered to Lothair in 1130, and in 1134
Frederick, and in 1135 Conrad, gave up the contest.

Schism of Innocent II. and Anacletus, 1130. — This
struggle was going on when the king was drawn into
the thick of the Italian quarrel.   Honorius II. died in
1130, and a doubtful and contested election followed.
The smaller body of cardinals elected Innocent II.,
the majority Anacletus II. ; the former made their
election first ; the latter in contempt of it, made theirs
at the canonical time.   Anacletus was supported by
the nobles of Rome and by the Normans of Sicily ;
Innocent relied for help on the party in the empire
which was now powerfully represented by Lothair ; he
sought assistance in France, and obtained it ; he then
applied to Lothair, crowned him king at Liege, and
obtained recognition from all the kings north of the
Alps.   In the company of Lothair and S. Bernard he
returned in triumph to Rome, where he bestowed upon
the former the imperial crown in the Lateran Church,
June 4, 1133, Anacletus being in possession of the
Vatican and the castle of S. Angelo.   The reward of
Lothair was to be the possession of the Countess Matilda's

inheritance ; this was actually yielded to him for life only, for an annual payment of 100 marks of silver. On his death they were to go to his son-in-law, Henry of Bavaria. But Lothair could not stay at Rome. Innocent retired with him and kept his court at Pisa. Anacletus ruled with the Normans in the South, and made his brother-in-law, Roger Wiscard of Sicily, a king ; it was not until 1136–37 that Lothair was able to attempt thoroughly to reinstate Innocent.

Lothair's Relations with the Normans of Sicily, 1137—*His Death.*—In 1136 he visited Italy again, upset the Lombard republics, but spared the cities of the Æmilian provinces at the request of Henry of Bavaria. The same duke as his general reduced the whole of North Italy, and advanced to Benevento which he took and restored to the Pope. Lothair himself proceeded as far as Apulia, the Normans being unprepared or fearful of encountering him ; but before a battle had been fought, he was compelled by the discontent of his forces to return, and contented himself with declaring Roger a public enemy and instituting a new duke—Reginald, a Norman baron. It was on this expedition that the Pandects were discovered at Amalfi by the Pisans. A quarrel ensued between Lothair and Innocent, both claiming to be suzerains of Apulia. On his return from Italy, leaving Anacletus in Rome, Lothair was taken ill amid the mountains above Trent, and died in a labourer's cottage in the Tyrol in great distress on the 4th of December 1137. This is nearly the whole of the history of his reign ;—his struggle with the Hohenstaufen and his Italian campaigns. Between the two latter, the stubborn brothers had given in and were received into favour by Lothair, Conrad being made standard-bearer of the empire.

Henry the Proud.—Lothair indeed does not seem to have contemplated the possibility of conveying the crown hereditarily, for he had no son; but he heaped on his son-in-law, Henry the Proud, the heir of the Bavarian Welfs and of the Tuscan Este's, the nephew of Welf II., the Countess Matilda's husband, and the heir of the Billungs of Saxony, all the power that he could. To him he gave the march of Tuscany as the reward of his successful generalship in Italy, and in the last years of his life his own Saxon possessions, the allods of the house of Nordheim and Brunswick, and the great fief of Saxony itself. The authority of Henry the Proud extended thus from the Weser almost to the gates of Rome, and his dominions were more than equal in extent to the German kingdom of the Karolings, Bavaria extending still over the whole of South Germany, east of the Lech, and Saxony being reunited in his person, in fiefs and allods, which had been separated since the time of the Emperor Otto. He was a brave man and a wise ruler, but Lothair took no direct means of obtaining for him the succession, which the jealousy of the minor princes was seen to begrudge him. Lothair was an old man for a king, about sixty-two at the time of his death, and had been a great warrior in his time.

Importance of Lothair's Reign.—His reign is chiefly memorable as a break into the continuity of the imperial opposition to the Papacy, and as the period of the foundation of what was subsequently the Welf party, opposed both religiously and secularly to the Ghibeline or Waiblingen party of the House of Hohenstaufen. The influence of the Welf family rested first on their enormous ancestral and feudal property; secondly, on the fact of their popularity and personal hold in Saxony, which was the stronghold of the independent anti-imperial or German party; and thirdly, on their faithful attachment, with the Saxons, to the Apostolic See. The Welfs themselves, although of Swabian origin and rising to eminence in Bavaria, never possessed the hearts of the Bavarians as they did those of the Saxons, with whom they were bound by the most ancient ties and the closest political sympathy.

Election of Conrad III., 1138.—Lothair was buried in his own estate between Brunswick and Helmstadt, at a monastery named Kaiserslutter. His only child was Gertrude, the wife of Henry of Bavaria. His policy seems to have been in internal matters to consolidate the power of the remaining princes; he raised the provincial Count of Thuringia to an hereditary princedom, still bearing the title of Landgraviate, and consolidated the Margraviates of Meissen and Lausitz; under his influence also the Dukes of Zähringen, also strong Welf partisans, acquired great power in Burgundy and Alsace. On the death of Lothair the imperial and royal insignia were left in the charge of Henry the Proud, who should have presented them to a diet before a new election could be made. Long before this, the succession was settled by surprise: the princes, afraid that he would claim the empire as his right, met at Coblentz in Lent, and in the presence of the papal legate, Cardinal Theodwin, elected Conrad of Hohenstaufen, Duke of Franconia, the younger brother of Frederick of Swabia. The see of Mainz was vacant; Conrad was crowned at Aix-la-Chapelle by the cardinal. A diet was summoned at Bamberg for Whitsuntide; there the Saxon princes, under the Empress Richenza, gave in their adhesion. On the

29th of June Henry the Proud surrendered the regalia at Regensburg, but declined to submit to Conrad and left the court in enmity. Conrad used sharp measures against him; condemned him to deprivation in a diet at Würzburg, and actually deprived him of all his fiefs at Goslar at Christmas. "Wonderful to say," adds Otto of Freising, "this most mighty prince, whose dominion extended from sea to sea, from Denmark to Sicily, came in a short time to such humiliation that, all Bavaria deserting him, he came into Saxony with only four companions." Bavaria was immediately bestowed by the triumphant Conrad on his half-brother, Leopold of Austria; Saxony was given to Albert the Bear, Margrave of Soltzwedel or Brandenburg; and Holstein was taken from his faithful friend, Count Adolf II. But the humiliation lasted not very long. The Saxons rose in his favour. In vain Conrad insisted that no prince should hold two duchies; Henry and Albert went to war, and the issue was in favour of Henry. He had recovered Saxony and was preparing to march into Bavaria when he died suddenly, not without suspicion of poison, on October 20, 1139, at Quedlinburg.

The Results of the Death of Henry the Proud, 1139.— Henry's only son was Henry, afterwards so famous as the Lion; he was now only ten years old, and unable of course to assert his claim to any part of his father's estates. His grandmother, Richenza, however, maintained his right to Saxony, and as long as she lived, Albert the Bear was unable to preserve even his own dominions. She died in 1141. In Bavaria, Welf, the brother of Duke Henry the Proud, attempted to make a party for his nephew, as for himself, and even attacked Conrad himself, whilst besieging Weinsburg in Swabia. A sharp struggle ensued, in which Welf was beaten, and which is memorable as the occasion on which the war-cries of Welf and Waiblingen were first heard. This was in 1140. Peace was not made until 1142, when Henry the Lion was invested with the duchy of Saxony; and Bavaria was given, with his mother, Gertrude, to Henry of Austria, another half-brother of Conrad. This arrangement led to a new war between this Austrian Henry and Welf, who now set up a claim to Bavaria for himself. Henry the Lion, as he grew up, made some attempts to recover that duchy from his stepfather, but he did not succeed in doing so whilst Conrad lived. Poor Welf, who was on all sides treated as an adventurer, saw more fortunate days, under Frederick Barbarossa, who was his nephew. His personal influence lay chiefly in Swabia itself which was governed by the young Frederick from 1147. Altogether the warfare amongst these cousins was not very vindictive, although it cost much blood of the fighting men, and wasted the strength of the empire. Conrad had enough to do; and what he did was not well done. Italy was altogether neglected. The Normans made Innocent II. a prisoner; he was compelled to crown Roger Wiscard, whom Lothair had declared a public enemy, king of Sicily. Yet Conrad harassed by Welf was unable to stir. Welf entered into alliance with Roger and was subsidised by him; and with Wardis, the usurping king of Hungary. Conrad beat Wardis, and at last in 1147 compelled him to give sureties for his good behaviour; but Welf it was impossible to catch.

The Second Crusade, 1147.—Such was the condition of affairs when S. Bernard came to Germany to preach the second Crusade. No one received him more heartily than Conrad, who declared that he, as well as the King of France, would undertake the expedition, and it should be one worthy of collective Christendom. For the time war ceased in Germany, everything and everybody was preparing for the pilgrimage. Even Henry the Lion was prevailed on by Conrad to suspend his claim on Bavaria until the return from Palestine. Early in 1147 the Crusade started from Nuremberg at Ascensiontide—Conrad at the head of the Germans, with Welf, Frederick, Henry of Austria, and many other princes. Before he went, he had his son Henry crowned king as his successor. The Crusaders marched through Hungary and Thrace to Constantinople. Before, however, Conrad reached Syria he lost most of his forces in Asia Minor, and was obliged to return to Constantinople for ships. Arrived in Palestine he found himself able to do nothing. The strength of the united armies, or what was left of them, was spent on the siege of Damascus; Conrad returned to Germany, having lost everything but his character as a brave warrior, in 1149.

Death of Conrad, 1152.—The rest of the interest of the reign depends on Roman affairs, and the revolution, religious, philosophic and political, produced in Italy by Arnold of Brescia. But Conrad was too busy to deliver Innocent from either the republicans or the Normans. Pope after Pope was chosen and bullied, but the great patron gave no sign. At last after the Crusade was over and the exhaustion consequent upon it a little recovered, Conrad prepared to go to Rome to accept the imperial crown, to punish rebellious republicans, and to extinguish the tyranny of the Normans. With this intention he came to

Bamberg early in 1152 to collect his forces; and there felt the inroads of his last disease. Poison of course was suspected. The Sicilian Normans had already a character for such a plan of getting rid of an enemy. At Bamberg on the 15th of February 1152 Conrad died. He had lost his son and elect successor Henry two years before ; his only other son was yet a child. The Saxons would be too strong for him. He named therefore Frederick of Hohenstaufen, his nephew, his successor and committed to him the imperial insignia.

Conrad's Character.—Much cannot be said about Conrad personally, but it is clear that, in spite of his political weakness, he was a man of ability and character. The Saxon and Bavarian influence in Germany was stronger than any that he, as emperor, or duke, or representative of the Franconian emperors, could bring against it. He was unable to master it at home, or to carry the influence of a united Germany abroad. Never since the time of Henry the Fowler had the German influence been so abased in Italy ; and the foolish Crusade, foolish that is for a prince in Conrad's circumstances, put a finishing stroke to the exhaustion of the kingdom. Conrad was a devoted adherent of S. Bernard ; he ruled the politics of Europe for peace, if not with much wisdom or justice ; and when he acted for himself showed the qualities of a brave man. But Conrad cannot be called a great king or even a great man. The results of the three reigns which have been so briefly characterised will be considered in their bearing on the condition of Germany under Frederick Barbarossa.

IMPORTANT DATES

Henry V., 1106–1125.
Border warfare in Germany, 1106–1111.
Henry's coronation at Rome, 1111.
Henry's struggle with Paschal, 1111–1118.
Henry's marriage with Matilda of England, 1114.
Death of Paschal, 1118.
The Concordat of Worms, 1122.
Henry's death, 1125.
Lothair II., 1125–1137.
Siege of Speyn by Lothair, 1129–1130.
Coronation of Lothair at Rome, 1133.
Lothair in Apulia, 1137.
His death in the Tyrol (Dec.), 1137.
Conrad III., 1138–1152.
Death of Henry the Proud, 1139.
Restoration of Saxony to Henry the Lion, 1142.
The second Crusade, 1147.
Death of Conrad on his return from the Crusade, 1152.

CHAPTER XI

The Empire on the Accession of Frederick Barbarossa, 1152.—If Frederick Barbarossa could have taken up the empire as it was left by Henry III., it is just within the verge of possibility that he might by his reign of nearly forty years have produced a change which would have materially affected Europe down to this day. But, if it had been so, it seems certain that it must have been not so much by extending the limits or vindicating the reality of imperial power, as by the creation of a thoroughly united and feudally organised kingdom in Germany. Great as were the changes within Germany, they were greater still outside of it. The Normans, from having been for three centuries the scourge of Europe from north to south, had become a civilised and splendidly civilised people, as civilisation then went. Instead of being known by mere piratic excursions on the coasts of the Mediterranean, they were now a recognised and centralised power in European affairs, were represented by two mighty insular kingdoms, and were by their participation in the Crusades claiming a position held as yet only by the most ancient mon-archies.

Condition of Italy.—In Italy, however, the German king found himself opposed not by the scattered Lombard principalities in Apulia, or by the officers of the antiquated empire in Calabria, powers which were hardly worth conquering and wholly insignifi-cant in their hostility, but by a compact and well organised feudal state, in possession of all that the strength of the north and the skill of the south could combine to give. By the assistance of a power like the Normans, the Papacy could make head against the emperor in person. Nay, without the assistance of the Normans, Gregory VII. had reduced the king of Germany to the condition of a suppliant vassal ; and the court of Rome never yet formally withdrew a single claim that she had made to secular dominion. For the best part of a century the relation of the two powers had been changed. Instead of the emperor acting as a patron of the Church, the Church was becoming the patron of the empire ; instead of the emperor being the reformer of the Church, the Church was attempting to reform the empire. Claims had been made and admitted, and favours had been asked and granted, that made the restoration of the old status virtually an impossibility. Even in the north of Italy, the country on which the yoke of German empire had always sat most uneasily, matters were more advanced towards a perpetual and successful resistance. The Lombard and Tuscan towns were quickly raising a fabric of republican independence on the basis of their old imperial municipalities. They were seeking strength by federation, and by mutual assistance insuring one another against the

damages of an unsuccessful quarrel. In the alliance
of the Papacy, or of the Norman king of Sicily, or
of any German prince who was disaffected towards
the reigning house, or by the subsidies of any European
prince who wanted a good word with the Pope, these
cities were acquiring internal strength and at the
same time political experience and a recognition in
the family of states. It is now clear that the term of
imperial dominion beyond the Alps was becoming
shorter; and that there were obstacles which had grown
up since the time of Henry III. which it would have
taxed his power as it did that of his descendant to
cope with.

The Political Situation in Germany.—Germany was
different. In the first place her frontier was more
defined, and her neighbours more dependent. The
claims of the French upon Lorraine had ceased;
and the whole of the old Lotharingian kingdom acknowledged the supremacy of the empire. On the
north the Danes were subservient, and the Obotrites,
Slavs, Wends, and Bohemians, Poles and Hungarians,
were content to accept a vassal relation compatible
with peace. Christianity and civilisation were gaining
hold faster and faster upon them, and the King of
Bohemia was become a prince of the German kingdom.
In Germany itself there was a lull of dynastic quarrels,
which is refreshing or the contrary, as the reader takes
pleasure or not, in unravelling the petty complications
of the interior of the kingdom. The concentration of
fiefs in the hands of one or two great princes has the
effect of simplifying these, and sometimes of extinguish-
ing them after a time or altogether. Conrad III. left
Germany not indeed united but in a condition to
become so; and, as regards strength, not so much

absolutely powerful as contingently so, on the absence and cessation of old causes of weakness. The Welf and Franconian parties were now all that were left to divide Germany. Frederick stood in exactly the same relation to both : his mother was sister to Duke Henry the Proud ; his father was brother to the Emperor Conrad. Conrad perhaps saw, or thought he saw, in Frederick one who would make the best and wisest use of the influence to which he was born, and one who might unite for ever North and South Germany in the bonds of friendship and political sympathy. On his deathbed he preferred his nephew Frederick as his successor to his own son ; and the choice was ratified by the opinion of Germany, the young Duke of Swabia being already known as a warrior, a statesman, and a Crusader. He was also popular and bound in the closest terms of affection and companionship with the hereditary representative of the Welfs, and he had no hereditary feuds of his own to cultivate.

Character of the Reign of Frederick Barbarossa.—The long reign of Frederick Barbarossa justified the choice. He made and kept a strong German kingdom, and, with the empire, he did the best that could be done. If he had devoted himself entirely to Germany he might have averted the fate of his family, and altered the face of Europe. This he did not do, and the pernicious hold upon Italy involved the breaking up, after his death, of all that he had effected. But although that is so, he certainly governed Germany more completely than it had been governed before ; and though unable to substitute the despotic for the feudal form of imperialism—unable, that is, to undo the work of the last century altogether—he was still able to substitute feudal order for feudal disorder, and by his own authority and good faith to keep his vassals, even the greatest of them, in their places. As it will be impossible with any minuteness to go into details in chronological order for this reign, it will be advisable first to clear the way by enumerating Frederick's Italian expeditions in which, as Hallam says, there is, for the general reader, the greatest part of the interest of the reign; then to trace the progress of the Welf and Waiblingen, Saxon and Swabian—the North and South German chronic quarrel — and around that group the chief German transactions of this very important reign.

The Position of Frederick Barbarossa on his Accession.— Frederick Barbarossa, then, was the son of Frederick the one-eyed Duke of Swabia, by Judith, the sister of Henry the Proud. His grandmother on the father's side was Agnes of Swabia, daughter of Henry IV.; his great-grandmother on the mother's side was Judith of Flanders, the widow of Tostig, sister-in-law of both Harold and William the Conqueror, and the line by which unmistakably the blood of both Charles the Great and the English Alfred runs through the veins of the royal houses of Europe. Agnes of Swabia had married, after her first husband's death, and her large family by Leopold, Margrave of Austria, were the most faithful adherents of the Swabian family. There was thus no great prince in Germany who was not closely allied with Frederick, and this alliance had been strengthened for the most part by their common participation in the miseries and glories of the second Crusade. By Conrad's advice Frederick was elected King of Germany on the 5th of March 1152 at Frankfort, unanimously : he was crowned at Aix-la-Chapelle on mid-Lent Sunday. He then travelled though Saxony and Bavaria, where he was crowned a second time at Regensburg, and sent to Rome to demand the imperial crown. His first exercise of authority was to settle peacefully the claims of three competitors to the crown of Denmark, and to appease the dissension between Henry the Lion and his rivals both in Saxony and in Bavaria. In these matters his two first years were spent, and in 1154 he made his first expedition into Italy.

His First and Second Expeditions to Italy, 1154-55, *and* 1158-62—*The Diet at Roncaglia,* 1155.—The memorable points of this expedition, are, *first,* the great diet held on the plain of Roncaglia, in which he reviewed the whole feudal and military force of the empire; his ravaging of the Milanese territory; his coronation at Pavia; his rejection of the claim of the Roman republic and refusal of money to the people; the condemnation and execution of Arnold of Brescia; his armed occupation of Rome, and coronation by Pope Hadrian IV., with the battle that took place on the coronation day, June 18, and the sack and plunder of Spoleto. Frederick returned to Germany by way of Trent and Bavaria in the autumn of 1155. A Polish war, troubles in Germany, the establishment of the duchy of Austria, and Henry's marriage with the heiress of Burgundy were the chief events between the first expedition and the second, which took place in 1158. This was provoked by the indefatigable perseverance of the Milanese, who had not only recovered from their losses, but resumed their tyrannical position with regard to the neighbour cities, which they had lost in 1154. This time he again ravaged the Milanese lands, and ordered the demolition of the city of Crema, although he spared Milan itself. He was then crowned at Monza, and held another diet at Roncaglia of the whole empire, the character of which was legal rather than military, as that of 1154 had been. He insisted on the vassals of Lombardy, both bishops and cities, surrendering their rights of regalia (Hallam, i. 372), and ordered the institution of an imperial magistrate or podesta to join with the elective consuls in the administration of the towns. He next collected the estates and rights of the Countess Matilda on behalf of his uncle Welf. This was followed by a quarrel with Pope Hadrian IV., who insisted on the restoration of the Countess Matilda's estates, the absolute dominion of Rome, and on other diminutions of the imperial rights. The Pope' was fortifying himself by a close alliance with the Normans and the Lombard towns, and the great quarrel with Milan followed. Then ensued the death of Hadrian IV., and the double election of Alexander III. and the Cardinal Octavian as Victor IV., the emperor recognising the latter. Contemporaneous with these events was the war in Lombardy, which had for one result the utter destruction of Milan in 1162, after a resistance lasting for three years. Frederick then returned to Germany after an absence of four years, and attempted to strengthen there and in Europe generally the party of the anti-Pope.

Frederick's Third (1163), *Fourth* (1167), *and Fifth* (1174) *Italian Expeditions—The Lombard League,* 1167.— Frederick's ·third Italian expedition was in 1163, and was tolerably pacific; the emperor saw doubtless that the Lombard cities were recovering themselves, and perhaps anticipated the struggle which was so shortly renewed. In 1167 he made his fourth Italian expedition, reduced Lombardy again to a state of exhaustion,

and placed the anti-Pope, Paschal III., on the papal
throne. The result of this expedition was bad; for
not only did the rival Pope, Alexander III. (1159–81),
excommunicate him and release his subjects from their
allegiance, but the Milanese and their confederates
harassed his army, greatly diminished by disease, to
such a degree that he was pursued from city to city,
obliged to make peace and had to make his escape
over the Alps with a small band of attendants. Five
years intervened before, in 1174, he again entered Italy.
The Lombard league, formed in 1167 under papal protection, had now become too strong for him. Till
April 1175 he besieged Alessandria, the capital or
representative city of the new league, which had been
founded in 1168 and frightened the Lombards into
negotiations for peace. This Peace of Montebello
did not last long; the incurable faithlessness of the
Italians provoked the emperor to the last pitch; he
collected the force of the empire—only his cousin
Henry the Lion refused to accompany him. He fought
without him and was thoroughly beaten at Legnano
in 1176—that was enough. Negotiations for peace
were opened with the Pope on the death of the
anti-Pope Calixtus and with the Lombards and Sicilians.
These were effectual, and the whole of the parties
were formally reconciled at Venice in July 1177.
There the emperor and Pope met and exchanged
compliments. The peace was more lasting and the
reconciliation more sincere than such things generally
are. Frederick and Alexander continued friends until
the death of the latter. But a desultory private warfare
was carried on among the nobles. Still Frederick kept
his peace with the cities, and although he had several
quarrels with the Popes, he only once again entered

Italy.[1] In 1186, he held a diet at Milan, and a council with the Pope at Verona, and married his son Henry to the heiress of Sicily. For all the details of these things the reader must consult Sismondi, Milman, and Hallam.

Henry the Lion.—During the whole of these transactions down to 1176 Henry the Lion, the Duke of Saxony, had been the most intimate companion and energetic assistant of the emperor. They were attached by close personal friendship. Frederick had shown himself a good friend to the Welfs. He immediately recognised Henry as Duke of Saxony and as having hereditary claims on Bavaria ; as early as 1154 he had shown his determination to do him justice, and summoned Henry of Austria, his stepfather, to plead his cause before the diet of the empire. Failing his appearance on the third or fourth summons, the diet at Goslar adjudged Bavaria to Henry the Lion ; Frederick compromised matters, however, by dividing the march of Austria from the duchy of Bavaria permanently, restoring the latter to Henry the Lion, and creating the other an independent dukedom. Before this, as early as 1153, he provided for his uncle Welf by enforcing his rights on Tuscany, and investing him himself with the fief of that marquisate. Welf still had considerable estates in Tuscany and Lombardy, derived from his ancestors of the house of Este, of which he was recognised in Italy as the head. He had a son Welf, who gained the affections of his Italian vassals and ruled in his stead until 1167. For seven years Henry the Lion grew in power and character ; he conquered, and that

---

[1] The Peace of Venice, 1177, with the Pope was, in 1183, followed by the Peace of Constance with the Lombard republics, which now became self-governing states.

permanently, the Slav population on the Elbe and south-west shores of the Baltic ; he built cities ; he founded bishoprics and churches ; he joined in the imperial expeditions ; he accepted, contrary to the policy of his Saxon forefathers, the emperor's side in the disputes with the Papacy. In 1156 he saved Frederick's life at Rome, was betrothed by his influence to Matilda of England in 1165, and was married in 1168. In 1172 he went on a magnificent pilgrimage to Jerusalem and spent his wealth, power, and statesmanlike skill in the civilisation and embellishment of Saxony, and especially of his allods of Brunswick. There is no doubt that his faithfulness to Frederick was sincere, and was a great cause of the emperor's strength and prosperity during these years. In 1160, when Frederick thought it wise to nominate a successor, he named after his own son, then a child, Henry the Lion as the most worthy.

Henry the Lion's Quarrel with the Emperor, 1180.—From the year 1167, which was the year of the death of the younger Welf, these relations became less friendly. Even whilst Henry the Lion was on his pilgrimage, the emperor it was said tampered with the Saxon lords ; but this he might easily do, without evil intention, for Henry had no children as yet, and his return from such an expedition was somewhat doubtful. Still the knowledge of these intrigues and the excommunication of Frederick and his allies by Alexander III., 1168, may have had some effect upon the duke on his return from his pilgrimage, for Henry was both religious himself and the representative of a religious school or party in Germany. But it can scarcely be doubted that the succession to the estates of Duke Welf produced the final coolness. Although this troublesome old man lived until 1195, he did not care to govern his Tuscan estates, and the regency went with the succession. He made his will first in favour of Henry the Lion, but either offended by him or persuaded by Frederick, who had now a young family to provide for, he changed his mind and gave the succession to him. This was perhaps the crowning offence with Henry. He would not waste his Saxon and Bavarian troops in winning in Italy the inheritance that he thought ought to have been his own, for the children of his cousin. Frederick had collected his forces for Italy in 1175 for the final humiliation of the Pope and of the Lombard towns. The only defaulter was his old friend and companion. Henry refused to join in the expedition. The emperor invited him to meet him at Chiavenna on the Lake of Como, and Henry met him. According to one account Henry insisted on receiving Goslar, one of the most important imperial towns in Saxony, as a fief, before he would stir ; this Frederick refused. Henry then offered to show all obedience to his cousin, but refused to join him in person. Then it is said that Frederick had recourse to entreaty, and even fell on his knees to pray him to consent. But Henry was obdurate, and did not even offer to raise up the suppliant emperor. For this he was never forgiven.

Disgrace of Henry the Lion, 1180.—Frederick went to Italy and was defeated at Legnano, and obliged subsequently to make peace and a truce with the cities, the Pope, and the Normans. Almost as soon as the breach was known, Henry became an object of persecution, especially by the imperialist bishops. The Archbishop of Cologne ravaged his Bavarian estates, and the Bishop of Halberstädt kept Saxony in an uproar. Afraid of exasperating the emperor, Henry contented himself with the simplest measures of defence and with complaints to Frederick of the unauthorised hostilities of his neighbours. In 1179 he met him at Speyer, and Frederick fixed the day of arbitration at Worms; but he showed such anger against his cousin on this occasion, reproaching him so violently and accusing him of complicity with the Italians, that Henry did not venture to attend. He was then summoned to Magdeburg, where many new accusations were brought against him in his absence. After an interview at Hadesleben, in which the emperor begged him to satisfy his enemies by submitting to a fine of 5000 marks, he was for the third time ordered to appear before the diet at Goslar. Here he was adjudged to have forfeited all his fiefs and honours by default. In a fourth assembly, held at Würzburg early in 1180, he was deprived, and shortly after at mid-Lent in that year, in a diet at Gelenhausen, the estates of which he was stripped were divided amongst the bitterest of his foes. This division was indeed a new partition of Germany, and caused a change in the face of the country which was never obliterated. Henry, it will be remembered, possessed Saxony and Bavaria as fiefs, and Brunswick and Lüneburg with a great part of the middle of Saxony allodially; on these allodial domains, of course, the dower of his wife Matilda was settled. Saxony was henceforth divided, Westphalia and Angria, the western third, were given to Philip of Heinsberg, Henry's most inveterate persecutor, as a fief to be joined to the archbishopric of Cologne. The eastern third, with the office of Duke of Saxony, was given to Bernard of Ascania, son of his father's enemy Albert the Bear, Margrave of Brandenburg, and ancestor of the existing reigning house of Anhalt. Bavaria also was divided in a council at Ratisbon.

The part which contains modern Bavaria from the Lech to the Austrian border was given with the title of duke to Otto of Wittelsbach, ancestor of the reigning house of Bavaria. The southern limb, the Tyrol, was erected into a duchy, called the duchy of Meran, for Count Berthold of Andechs, from whom the house of Austria descends by females; this duke held also Istria and Dalmatia and several important estates in the south of Germany, which were known as the Vogtland, *Terra Advocati*—the origin of which is not clear. The old Welfic estates the emperor took into his own hands.

The End of the Quarrel.—Henry did not yield without a struggle. Lübeck was only surrendered to the emperor in person, and dates from this event (1181) its existence as an imperial city. Brunswick held out against the emperor so long and manfully that he was obliged to retire from it. By earnest pleading and making the most of his legal position, Henry was saved from entire ruin. His allodial estates and Welfic property were restored to him, and he was banished for three years. This alleviation of the first sentence is said by the English historians to have been won by intercession of his father-in-law, Henry II. of England, into whose dominions he retired to spend his exile. He returned in 1185, and immediately attempted to recover his authority over Saxony. In this he failed, and his presence in Germany continued to be irksome to the emperor. At last on the arrangements made in 1187 for departure on the Crusade, Frederick offered him a choice of three things: *either* to accept his restoration under some very stringent restrictions, *or* to join in the pilgrimage, *or* to go again into exile. He preferred the latter alternative, and remained in exile until he heard of the departure of Frederick. The rest of his history belongs to another reign, but it may be added here that after a short struggle with Henry VI., he submitted to him and died in 1195.

The Results of the Overthrow of Henry the Lion—His Death, 1195.—One of Henry the Lion's sons was made Count Palatine of the Rhine by Henry VI.; another, Otto, was emperor as Otto IV.; another, William of Winchester, preserved Brunswick and Lüneburg in the Welfic line and these were constituted a duchy by the Emperor Frederick II. in 1227. The importance of the catastrophe of Henry the Lion to German history can hardly be exaggerated; it produced a greater change on the map than the extinction of the house of Hohenstaufen itself did. More than a third of Germany was subdivided, and a great number of nobles who had been subject feudally to the dukes became immediate tenants of the empire. Another result was the bringing into prominence of a class of nobles which had hitherto stood in the background. The dukes of the five nations no longer engrossed the highest title. There were dukes of Zähringen, Meran, Austria, and Carinthia. The old duchies were diminished in size and in prerogative. Some of them were disappearing. Saxony was now little more than a margravate. The margraves of Brandenburg were coming into prominence and the landgraves of Hesse and Thuringia, relieved from the overshadowing might of the Saxon dukes, were acting as chief feudatories. The County Palatine of the Rhine, however, was not yet constituted as a hereditary office, and the domains of the emperor or king were of considerable extent. The imperial cities as imperial cities continue to rise, the overshadowing power of the provincial governments being less than before.

The Power of Frederick Barbarossa.—The fall of Henry the Lion is interesting as a proof of the completeness of the rule which Frederick Barbarossa was by his strength, justice, and policy enabled to exercise on the country which so many of his predecessors had been content to rule merely as umpires. It was not as if Henry the Lion were without friends. He was the most influential man in Germany after the emperor, and he was the traditional head of a political party. Yet his friends made no effort to avert the sentence that was passed against him; the only resistance to the carrying out of it was offered on his own allodial lands. The reign of law under Frederick was shown to be complete; and the feudal system shown to be advanced to that stage in which every vassal is compelled to acknowledge the authority of the suzerain and to discharge his own lawful liabilities. Nor is it much less interesting as a matter of character. It is one of those cases in which we can take a fair enough judgment without acquitting or condemning either party. Frederick had been a great benefactor to Henry, and Henry had been a most faithful friend and servant of Frederick. But the favours which Frederick had shown him were of such sort as would seem to Henry merely acts of justice; he had restored to him what had been the authority and estates of his father and mother. Henry's service to Frederick would seem just as much to the emperor a matter of rightful obedience in a vassal to his lord. Henry might easily demand a new guerdon for a new service. Frederick might easily expect the same new service to be done as a piece of the long-due and long-tried gratitude. But the breach once made could never be repaired. The enemies of Henry were too earnest to relax their hold on the imperial mind, and, if Frederick had wished to pardon, too large a number of princes were interested in the final crushing of the great Saxon dominion.

Frederick's Marriage with Beatrice of Burgundy, 1156.— The remaining acts of Frederick's long reign which seem interesting or important to Germany must now be noticed. The wife of Frederick Barbarossa, to whom (after being divorced from Adelheid of Vohburg, on the ground of consanguinity) he was married in 1156, was Beatrice, the daughter of Reinhold, Count of Burgundy. On the death of Reinhold, the inheritance fell to Beatrice, and Frederick took occasion by it to recover his authority not only in the free county, but in the rest of the kingdom of Burgundy, which had been placed by Lothair under the rule of the Duke of Zähringen as a part of the empire. Frederick resumed this territory, leaving to the duke that portion only which is embraced in modern Switzerland, and out of which, on the extinction of the family in 1218, were formed the estates noble, municipal, and ecclesiastical from which the Swiss republics sprang. Frederick was not, however, crowned King of Arles until 1178, when that ceremony was gone through, Beatrice being also crowned Queen of Burgundy at Vienne. From this marriage sprang several sons ; Henry, afterwards king and emperor ; Frederick, Duke of Swabia, who died soon after his father on the Crusade ; Conrad, Duke of Franconia, who succeeded his brother in Swabia and died soon after ; Philip of Swabia, the competitor of Otto IV.

for the empire, who was murdered by Otto of Wittelsbach at Bamberg; and Otto, to whom the free county
of Burgundy, his mother's estate, went. Frederick
did no more, in providing for these, than retain for
them the hereditary duchies which had been long
vested in the family, Franconia and Swabia, the
latter of which he himself had held, and the former
of which, having been held by Frederick of Rothen-
burg, son of the Emperor Conrad, fell in in 1167.
He had also possessed Swabia from the time of the
emperor's accession. The younger children, it will
be observed, were not provided for out of the forfeiture
of Henry the Lion, although some colour might have
been found for the proceeding in their descents
from the Welfs.

His Policy to the Slavs—The Great Council at Mainz,
1184.—The obscurest parts of the reign of Frederick
are those, of course, which are not illustrated by the
Italian or Welfic quarrels; and they extend from
1168 to 1173. In 1169 he had his eldest son Henry,
then five years old, crowned king at Aix-la-Chapelle,
but his whole efforts were probably being concentrated during these years on preparing for a new
attack upon Italy, and few particulars of other interest
are recorded. The years 1181-85 are also a lull;
in 1181 he admitted the princes of the Slavs to a
place in the number of German princes, thus leading
to the formation of the duchy of Pomerania, although
many years intervened before the Saxons and Slavs
were content to be dependent on the same rulers.
In 1184 a great court was held at Mainz from which
the appointment of the great offices of the empire
is understood to date. At this court the King of
Bohemia acted as cupbearer, the Duke of Saxony as

marshal, the Count Palatine as steward, and the Margrave of Brandenburg as archchamberlain. These offices remain finally in the hands of these princes; why Franconia, Swabia, and Bavaria were excluded does not appear. The Count Palatine at the time was Conrad, the emperor's brother, the Dukes of Franconia and Swabia were his sons. The assembly on this occasion included all the important princes and representatives of the kingdoms of Europe, and the period may be regarded as the culmination of the personal power and influence of Frederick.

Frederick's Eastern Expedition, 1189-90, *and Death*, 1190.—In 1188 Frederick took the Cross and involved in that fatal measure his son Frederick and a vast number of the princes and prelates of the empire. The expedition started from Regensburg on the feast of St. George, 1189. Frederick opened the expedition by sending a formal defiance to Saladin to meet him in the following November in the field of Zoan. In this Frederick writes as emperor and representative of all that is great in Roman, all that is varied and famous in his own national, history and dominion. Saladin's answer, or one made for him, is also preserved. Frederick pursued the old route of the Crusaders through Hungary and Thrace to Constantinople ; at Philippopolis he wintered and learned, as he had done forty years before, the irreconcilable enmity and incurable perfidy of the Greeks of Byzantium. In the spring he moved down carefully through Asia Minor, defeated the Seljuk Sultan of Iconium, and took his city. Going on thence, he was drowned in the Calycadnus or Salef, in which he was, according to one account, swimming, according to another, crossing on horseback. His son Frederick led the Crusaders as far as Antioch and there died. Frederick himself was buried partly at Antioch, the bones at Tyre ; and I believe they were never removed. There he lies still, it may be, in an unknown grave, the best and bravest and mightiest of the German Cæsars. But his people long looked for him to come again, and would not believe him lost. Still, according to popular German romance, in which it is hard to tell how much is tradition and how much genuine imagination, how little false sentiment, he sits in a cave either in the Harz, or in the Salzburg mountains, his beard grown through the stone table, but not dying, only awaiting the time when Germany shall be in her deadliest need, when he will rise with an earthquake and set his people again as in his own days. It is to be feared that if the need of a deliverer were the test of the truth of the story, it must go for no more than the same belief about the British Arthur.

Frederick's Character.—To one who comes to work at the original historians there is something lovable as well as admirable about Frederick Barbarossa ; something that there is in the great Charles without the full admiration that Frederick inspires. We get the full beauty of the German character in its strength, its purity, its kindness and patience, its gentleness and good faith, coupled with the lion-like strength and valour, the magnificence, the civilised and humanised, knightly deportment of the medieval cavalier. He was eloquent and skilled in languages, a brave soldier, an experienced warrior, a just judge, a sound and temperate politician, and had all the strong attachments and a dash of the romance of boyhood. There is something very grand, but not after the grandeur of the nineteenth century, in the spectacle of the old lion, having made peace at home and bound all quarrel-some people to it by oath, going forth into a strange land on the Lord's battles. We almost feel glad that he died before he suffered defeat, or saw as he must in all probability have seen had he lived, the ruin of the Frank kingdom, the destruction of his German soldiers, the imminent risk of all Christendom, the sad shame, and disease and disappointment of the Third Crusade.

IMPORTANT DATES

Frederick I. (Barbarossa), 1152-1190.
Frederick in Italy. Diet of Roncaglia, 1154.
Coronation of Frederick in Rome, 1155.
Diet at Besançon, 1157.
Frederick again in Italy, 1158-1162.
Destruction of Milan, 1162.
Frederick in Italy, 1163.
Diet at Würzburg, 1165.
Frederick at Rome. Formation of the Lombard League, 1167.
Frederick besieges Alessandria, 1174-1175.
Battle of Legnano, 1176.
Peace of Venice, 1177.
Quarrel with Henry the Lion, 1179-1181.
Peace of Constance, 1183.
The Great Council at Mainz, 1184.
Frederick starts on the Third Crusade, 1189.
His death, 1190.

CHAPTER XII

The reign of Henry VI., 1190–97—His marriage, 1195—The attempt
to make the imperial dignity hereditary — Philip of Swabia
crowned king—Otto of Saxony also crowned king as Otto IV.—
Death of Philip, 1208—Otto IV. emperor—Frederick II.
crowned king, 1215—His death, 1250—The geographical and national
divisions of Germany—The connection between England and
Germany—The government of Germany—The German dukedoms—Growth of the hereditary idea—Gradual extinction of the
dukedoms—The outlines of modern Germany to be seen in the
Middle Ages—The relations of Germany and Italy.

THIS chapter will contain (1) an extremely brief sketch
of the course of events in the reigns of Henry VI., Otto
IV., and Frederick II., and (2) a mere general view of
the progress that has been made, in the development
of German national life since the days of Charles the
Great.

The Reign of Henry VI., 1190–97.—Frederick Barbarossa had taken measures, before he left Germany,
for making the empire hereditary in his own house,
and the measures were so far successful that Henry VI.
saw himself on his father's death without a rival. After
a short struggle with Henry the Lion, the result of
which was the submission and restoration of the latter
to his allodial estates, the rest of the life of Henry
VI. was devoted to Italy, with short and not very important exceptions. There he had by his marriage
with Constance, the aunt of King William the Good,
obtained a right, although not an undisputed one, to
the Norman kingdom ; to secure this right he sacrificed

the interests of Germany, and transmitted it to his son
—a fatal inheritance. After the submission of Henry
the Lion, Henry VI. proceeded to Italy, where, after
being crowned emperor by Celestine III. at Easter
1191, he marched against Tancred, his Sicilian competitor ; he lost his forces by pestilence, and his wife,
Queen Constantia, was taken prisoner. Whilst he was
engaged in the pacification of Germany and securing
the imperial crown, Richard I. of England had wintered
in Sicily on his way to Palestine, and after a sharp
quarrel had concluded a close alliance with Tancred.
It was soon after Richard's departure that Henry VI.'s
unfortunate expedition took place. Henry could not
forgive Richard for treating with his rival, and took
advantage of his capture by Duke Leopold in December
1192 to have his revenge of him. The same year
Tancred died, and the death of his son, either shortly
before or immediately afterwards, left Sicily open to
Henry's claims. After spending some time in Germany
treating with Richard, bestowing on him the kingdom
of Arles, and, according to a rumour, extorting from
him the homage of a vassal for the crown of England,
he released him. He then descended into Sicily, and
was crowned with Queen Constantia at Palermo in
December 1195. The several campaigns by which he
completed his conquest and the cruel measures he took
to keep it, need not be described. It is a matter for
regret that it was by German blood that they were
won and with German servants that the conquests were
held. After several severe struggles Henry had succeeded in making himself the master, when he died
in 1197, leaving only the little child Frederick, now
three years old. All that is known of Henry VI. leads
to the conclusion that he was the degenerate son of a

noble father : he was cruel, arbitrary, and faithless, avaricious and tyrannical. Still under him Germany had good peace ; he chose to be conciliatory rather than severe with the Saxons and with the Welf family ; one son of Henry the Lion he made Count Palatine of the Rhine ; but the inheritance of Duke Welf of ·Tuscany, which fell in in 1195, he bestowed on his brother Philip, whom soon after he made Duke of Swabia.

The Imperial Dignity to be Hereditary. — His other measures are of little consequence, with one notable exception : he enacted, how or when is not exactly known, but doubtless in a diet which he had propitiated by establishing the hereditary descent of all fiefs for the future, that the imperial dignity itself should be hereditary, not bestowed by election, but devolving upon the nearest male heir of the last emperor. As a consequence of this enactment Henry annexed his wife's dominions, Naples and Sicily, to the empire. The consent of the bishops to this was purchased by other concessions ; and the act was allowed by fifty-two princes. But the Saxon nation refused consent, and Henry was obliged to content himself with the election of his son Frederick as King of the Romans. There is no doubt that Henry VI. had the full idea of the imperial character as world governing, and was ambitious of securing the reality in Europe at least. Such was the motive of his dealings with Richard ; and the exercise of his supreme prerogative may be seen in his appointment of Amalric of Lusignan to the kingdom of Cyprus.[1] Contemporary historians tell us that Henry VI. took some steps towards acquiring the imperial crown of Byzantium, an object

---

[1] Frederick Barbarossa had already raised the Prince of Armenia to the status of royalty.

of either ambition or avarice to his Sicilian predecessors ; but the shortness of his reign prevents us
from either realising his ideas or of estimating the
ability he possessed of carrying them out. His great
act, of making the empire hereditary, was entirely futile ;
it was rejected by the Saxons and annulled by the Pope
as infringing or limiting the right of the successors of
St. Peter to recognise the emperor by consecration and
coronation.

Philip of Swabia crowned King, 1198.—The result of
the attempt and of the coincident minority of Frederick,
was to produce in Germany such a struggle for the
supremacy as had not been seen since the days of the
Karlings, either for length or vehemence. Philip of
Swabia (the brother of Henry VI.) was the guardian
of the young Frederick, named by his father before
his death, and Philip naturally determined to take the
course most adapted to secure the permanent union
of the dominions of his brother ; he procured the recognition of Frederick by the princes and of himself
as guardian or defender of the empire. This, however,
displeased the Pope, Innocent III., under whose influence
the bishops of Germany, assisted by those of the princes
who were hereditarily opposed to the Hohenstaufen,
offered the imperial crown first to Duke Berthold of
Zähringen. Berthold refused, being bribed it was said
by Philip ; and the princes of the Waibling or Hohenstaufen party, who had hitherto supported Frederick,
offered the empire to Philip himself. He was crowned
king at Mainz on the Sunday after Easter.

Otto of Saxony crowned King as Otto IV.—The Pope
at once refused to recognise Philip's coronation ; the
Archbishops of Cologne and Trèves, bought with English
money by Richard I., and encouraged by the adhesion

of the Pope, in conjunction with the Count Palatine Henry, son of Henry the Lion, who belonged to the Welf party, at last elected Otto of Saxony, brother of the Palatine and nephew of the English king. This the Pope confirmed, Otto was crowned king July 4, 1198, at Aix-la-Chapelle. Again the Church and the secular princes are opposed to one another ; North Germany to South, Saxony to Swabia. Neither of the competitors was in possession of great resources, and the struggle though long was desultory. Otto supported himself by the aid of his English uncles and his hereditary estates ; Philip by the alliance with France, always the supporter of the Hohenstaufen, as England was of the Saxon interest, by his marriage with the Byzantine Irene, and by the waste of the hereditary property and ducal authority in Swabia. The subsequent liberties, immunities, and peculiar tenures of the Swabian nobles date from this epoch of Philip's extravagance, although their immediate relation to the empire dates from the extinction of the family.

Death of Philip, 1208, *Otto IV. Emperor*, 1208.—Philip had very nearly reduced Otto to submission, or at least to a compromise when in 1208 he was murdered at Bamberg for a private grudge. His character is pleasanter far than that of Henry VI., but he had only the good qualities of his brother without the great ones. His death opened the way for Otto's advancement ; this time he was unanimously chosen by the princes at Halberstadt. At Frankfort at Martinmas he received the imperial insignia, and betrothed himself to Beatrice, the daughter of Philip, whose death he next year avenged by the forfeiture of all the possessions of the murderer. Otto of Wittelsbach was killed by Henry

of Pappenheim, the marshal of the imperial court. The
Pope, of course, was glad enough to confirm the title
of Otto, who went into Italy and was crowned by
Innocent III. in October 1209. The friendship did not
bear the test of acquaintance. Otto as emperor adopted
measures for the recovery of all the imperial rights in
Italy; the inheritance of the Countess Matilda was
taken in hand; nay the investiture of bishops was
claimed and exercised. Innocent, who at this very
time was contending with John in England on the
same point, was not likely to yield it to Otto without
struggling. But for a time Otto was all powerful; the
Swabian line was extinct, all but the child Frederick,
and he was safe for some years. Otto even reduced
Apulia and entered into negotiation with the Sicilians.
But this Innocent III. would not endure; he determined not to be beaten by a man whom he had, so
to speak, placed on the throne; in Holy Week, 1211,
he excommunicated him. Otto had no ability as a
ruler; he had offended the Germans by his absence
from Germany, he offended the Italians by his oppressive measures, the nobles by taxation, the bishops
by humiliation. The excommunication as usual was
followed by a reaction in Germany.

Frederick of Hohenstaufen Elected King of Germany,
1211.—The prelates on Ascension Day, 1211, met at
Nüremburg, and in conjunction with the Swabians
determined to offer the throne to the young Frederick.
After some resistance the Pope confirmed the election.
Frederick, now seventeen, but a married man and a
father, the ablest man of the age, "Stupor mundi," as
his predecessor Otto III. had been "Mirabilia mundi,"
accepted the offer against the advice of his friends at
home. He started like a knight-errant; by August he

was in Swabia; in December he was elected at Frankfort. Otto was again only King of the Saxons. The struggle lasted three or four years. The battle of Bouvines in 1214 wrecked Otto; England could give him no more help. Philip Augustus was the firm supporter of Frederick, who in 1215 was crowned king at Aix-la-Chapelle. Making the best of a bad matter the emperor retired to Brunswick, where he maintained himself little molested by Frederick until his death in 1217.

Summary of Frederick II.'s Reign, 1215-1250.—Of the early glories, the errors, misfortunes, crimes of Frederick II. much has been written. Of his treatment by Honorius III. and Gregory IX. it is impossible to write with patience; all know the story of the Crusade—how the emperor was excommunicated first for not going, then for going; then disgraced for the peace he had made with the Saracens; forced into war with the Pope, made a subject of a crusade by the Papacy; excommunicated again by Alexander IV.; deposed in the Council of Lyons in 1245. Henry Raspe, Landgrave of Thuringia, the Pfaffen-könig, for a year only made head against him; William of Holland as Anti-Cæsar had no better luck. But after thirty years of strife Frederick was worn out, tired, it may well be, of life itself; after an interval of three years of inactivity he died, only fifty-six years old, in 1250. The fortunes of his house fell with him, and the empire itself may be deemed to have collapsed at the same time. For a short time attempts were made to hold Italy for his children, but the inveterate hostility of the Popes and the pertinacious hold of Charles of Anjou, with the loss of the French influence, rendered their case hopeless,

and they were extinguished in the person of Conradin
in 1268. The events that led to, and the results
that flowed from, the fall of Frederick II. must now
be left.

The Geographical and National Division of Germany.—
In previous chapters an attempt has been made to
describe the geographical and national divisions of
Germany; and in the thirteenth century as well as
in the tenth the division between north and south,
Saxony and Swabia, or Saxon and Bavarian, is still
the line of demarcation between two great parties, two
national and religious parties. The Saxon or northern
nationality has always been in alliance with the Church
and the Papacy; but it has always been a question
whether that alliance was not rather a consequence
than a cause of the jealousy between north and south.
The right conclusion seems to be that, although the
Saxon nobles were a religious and strongly Catholic
body, they were made weapons of papal policy rather
by their antagonism to the southern nations than
merely by their love for the Pope. The Saxon
emperors and their successors in the government
of Saxony, the Billungs and the Welfs, were more
strongly Saxon than the other houses were either
Franconian or Swabian; and this has been explained
by going in detail into the descent of the great
Saxon heritages and dwelling on their allodial, *i.e.*
national, as opposed to a feudal, beneficial, or otherwise imperial tenure.

The Connection between England and Germany.—
With the Saxon emperors and dukes it is that the
connection of England and Germany is chiefly
apparent. Otto I. married an English princess;
Henry II. the last of the Saxon line was the pro-

tector of Edmund Ironside's children; Henry the
Lion was son-in-law of Henry II. The alliance of
the Franconian emperors was rather with the Normans
than with the Saxons; *i.e.* it was rather a dynastic
than a national connection; it is exemplified in the
marriage of Henry III. with Gunhilda, the daughter
of Canute, and of Henry V. with the daughter of
Henry I. Under Henry II., the first national king
of England, the old national alliance with Saxony
recurs again; his daughter married Henry of Saxony;
their son Otto, by English money, became king and
afterwards emperor. Two of the children of John
come in contact with German history: Isabella, the
wife of Frederick II., and Richard, who himself was
King of Germany for many years during the inter-
regnum in the empire. But there was no national
feeling in this matter; Richard was regarded in both
lands with indignation rather than with pride. But
the influence of England on the Continent was exercised on different grounds from merely dynastic ones,
from the twelfth century downwards, although it
may have been considerably affected by such connections in taking the direction that it did. The
struggle of Henry II. with Alexander III. and Becket,
brought him into strange alliances. At one moment
he was committing himself with Frederick Barbarossa
to the recognition of an anti-Pope, intriguing with the
King of Sicily, and actually giving money to enable
the Lombard allies to fortify themselves against
Frederick, on the understanding that they should
constrain or persuade the Pope to depose Becket.

Besides the unity of interest between the Saxons
and the Popes, eternised by the Welf and Waiblingen
quarrels, the fact must not be left out of sight that,

whilst the elective character of the empire made it an object with the ambitious princes of Germany to keep the kingdom of Germany, which was less distinctly elective, in union with the empire, it would have been very much more for the benefit of the people that the German king should stay at home and extend the borders and execute the laws and develop the resources of his own dominions. The kingdom of Italy and the empire were hateful to the best sort of Germans ; to the princes they were valuable as distracting the power and weakening the oppressive strength of their suzerain. Hence the early murmurings of the Saxons even against their Saxon kings, and the frequent rivalry of the younger branch of the family with the elder. This had vanished after the Germans became entirely reconciled to the idea of the empire as the right of their elective king. And there is no doubt that the true instinct of Germany was strongest in the north, and the instinct of imperialism stronger in the south.

The Government of Germany.—Closely connected with the geographical division and territorial party questions, is that of government. The government of Germany, or rather the subordinate parts of the government, has been traced through several distinct phases. Under Charles the Great, until he becomes emperor, the several nations whom he governed retained their individuality, and he calls himself King of the Saxons and Lombards whom he had conquered, as well as of the Franks whom he governed by hereditary right. As emperor even he does not include all his titles to the obedience of the many nations of his subjects in any œcumenical title, but setting the imperial dignity, which was precarious, as a sort of crowning stone to the pyramid of his honours, he retains the mention of the nations severally in his royal style. Whatever plans he or Lewis after him may have had for the consolidation of the several kingdoms under an imperial elder brother, they were thrown to the wind by the treaty of Verdun, and from that time the French kingdom was independent for ever of the empire, Italy and Lorraine being at a later period reduced to much the same relation as they had held before. Still the several nations were distinct kingdoms; the King of Germany ruled over a sort of confederation of sub-kingdoms; the sub-kingdoms were separable amongst his sons, just as the kingdoms in France had been under the Merovingians, but they had retained their boundaries and their laws, their peculiarities of manners and dialects more strongly than the divided kingdoms of France had done, which were indeed often merely arbitrary arrangements, indicating no physical or even historical distinction between the divided nations. The separability of the German kingdoms was an acknowledged fact under the sons of Lewis the German; and it was not altogether extinct under the Saxon line of emperors, the constant effort of both Bavaria and Alemannia being to exalt their dukes into the station of kings. The result of this long-continued separability of the nations, and of the concentration of national feeling by the same means, produced that definiteness of geographical division and interest on which comment has been made.

The History of the German Dukedoms.—The internal history is chiefly made up of the struggles of the four or five nations under their dukes. These dukes were the deputies of the German king, entitled to take the lead in war and to govern the judicial proceedings of the nation over which they were set, subject to the visitations of the imperial or royal *missus*, and subordinating to their jurisdiction the bishops, who often were temporal as well as spiritual rulers, and the counts or *grafs* who were more especially judicial rulers of the several *gaus*, or shires as we should call them, into which the dukedoms were divided. So long as the nations were divisible, there was no thought of appointing hereditary dukes—to have done this would have been simply to prepare the way for the king or his posterity to be ousted, as had been the case with the Merovingians, and was also with the Karolings in France. The early dukes were simply regionary, beneficiary, or official.

Growth of the Hereditary Idea.—The hereditary succession appears first among the counts, many of whom no doubt owed their position as counts to the possession of allodial estates which set them beyond rivalry or competition in their own *gaus*. Once become hereditary the position of count was more permanent than that of beneficial duke, and placed its owner in a relation of rivalry to his superior. It has been already noticed, for instance, how in Franconia the authority of a beneficiary duke was liable to be defied by the hereditary Counts of Bamberg; and how in Saxony, the hereditary lords of Nordheim, Brunswick, and Lüneburg were almost independent of the dukes, and struggled for the nomination in a vacancy. If, however, the hereditary power of the counts was a great drawback on the jurisdiction of the beneficiary dukes, what was the result when the dukedoms also became hereditary? It ought to have had the effect of subordinating the counts as hereditary vassals of the dukes, just as it was in France, or as it tended to be.

P

But in point of fact it was not, for the emperors hesitated to commit to dukes, when they became *de facto* if not *de jure* hereditary, the same extensive rights as representatives of the Sovereign which they had held as beneficiaries. So, although the jurisdiction of the hereditary Dukes was clearer and more wieldy, it was not so extensive nor so summary as before. The tendency of this was to break up the interior unity of the nationalities. They were less at one in themselves, although they might be equally opposed to each other. Saxony was no longer one government, but the Saxons were as distinct as ever from the Swabians. This tendency has been traced in the history of the Billung dukes, and the union of Saxony again under the Welfic dukes was regarded as a return to the earlier type of national oneness, and to the more extended substantive authority of the dukes. The result, however, proved that such a reconstitution had failed; Saxony fell to pieces at the forfeiture of Henry the Lion, and Bavaria as well as Saxony was broken up by the later policy of Frederick Barbarossa.

Gradual Extinction of the Dukedoms.—The subdivision of the national duchies never obliterated the old national distinctions, for a Swabian is still a Swabian, and a Bavarian a Bavarian ; and the diminution of the jurisdiction of the dukes as imperial officers opened the way for the aggrandisement of the lower orders of nobility, of the bishops, the monasteries, and the municipal estates. Imperial cities were left standing monuments of independence in the midst of hostile dukedoms. Bishops and monasteries acquired by purchase or privilege the rights of imperial officers over their own estates ; and the counts rose in importance

as the dukes approached more nearly their own level.
When once a dukedom fell into abeyance, or its holder
as emperor or king wasted by subdivision the rights
and demesnes appurtenant to it, it became a mere
honorary jurisdiction; each count was, as the Dukes
had been, all powerful on his own land: he could
purchase privileges and immunities as well as the
churches and towns could do; or he might undertake
the office of advocate of a monastery, or of burgrave
of a town, and so subordinate all the elements of
political life within his reach to his own personal and
hereditary rule. In this way the royal house of Prussia
rose; beginning by being Counts of Hohenzollern, they
obtained the hereditary burgraviate of Nüremberg,
rose upon that to be margraves, on that to be electors,
dukes, and kings. With the extinction of the dukedoms
(and in the thirteenth century they became extinct
by either death or subdivision), great numbers of the inferior counts became immediately dependent on the
empire and petty kings whenever the empire was vacant
or the emperor weak. And this state of things continued
until the defeasance of the empire under Francis II. and
the repartition caused partly by Napoleon and partly by
his conquerors in 1815. The measures of Napoleon had
tended to the re-formation of Germany into compact
kingdoms; those of the allies broke up the kingdom he
had created in the north, that of Westphalia, into its
former constituents; and leaving nothing strong enough
to resist the dominion of Prussia, led not remotely to
the present state of affairs in Germany.

Growth of Independent Jurisdictions in Germany.—Not
only was the number of independent jurisdictions increased by the subdivision and extinction of the national
dukedoms, it was for a long period constantly in-

creasing by the accretion of territory on the north
and east from the Danes, the Wends, the Slavs, the
Moravians, the Czechs, the Poles, the Hungarians,
and the south Slavonic races or semi-Romaic in Istria
and Dalmatia. For the sway of the Ottos, unpalatable
as it may be to Italian nationality, extended down the
east of the Adriatic for some distance. All these accretions were formed into marches or margraviates—
those of Stade, of Saltwedel, of Brandenburg, or Lausitz,
or Meissen, of Moravia, of Austria, some of which
grew in time into states which have eclipsed the glory
of the earlier nations. Later on were formed marches
on the other border ; the Margraves of Baden governed
the borders between Germany and Lotharingia or afterwards France. These Margraves would be subject to
the beneficiary dukes of the nation they protected,
but whether they ever acknowledged more than an
honorary dependence on the hereditary ones may be
doubted. Witness the constant struggles between the
Welfic dukes and Saxony with the Margraves of Brandenburg, and of Bavaria with the Margraves of Austria.

Thuringia, Meissen, Hesse, and Alsace.—Besides these
lands there were a few portions of territory lying
between the separate nations which originally had
been border kingdoms and should have subsided into
marches, but, owing to the union of the nations under
the German king, escaped that character. Such were
Thuringia between Saxony and Franconia, and Meissen
between Saxony and Bavaria. These territories were
sometimes appurtenant to one and sometimes to another
of the duchies. Franconia, which was a small duchy,
was sometimes augmented with the administration of
Thuringia, and, after Thuringia was attached to Saxony,
with that of Carinthia and even Lorraine. Ultimately

Thuringia was made an independent fief under a land-grave, a sort of intermediate honour between a count and a duke, but equal in actual power to either. The Landgraviates of Hesse and Thuringia, sometimes united sometimes divided, gave many powerful ministers to Germany, and sometimes supplied a candidate for the empire. The landgraviate of Alsace, dismembered from the duchy of Alemannia, was the original dignity of Rudolf of Hapsburg, the founder of the Austrian line of emperors.

The Foundation of Modern Germanic Divisions laid in the Middle Ages.—In this way, in the very heart of the early Middle Ages, was laid the foundation, and the outlines drawn, of the Germany of to-day. Historically the petty divisions and insignificant governments of Germany as they existed before 1866 were respectable and even venerable ; for they showed that they had not failed in retaining the affections of many genera-tions of subjects, and that no tyranny has prevailed where so slight pressure would have forced them together. Powerless for war, they were powerful in peace, and centres of civilisation tending greatly to the cultivation of internal resources. With these ad-vantages they had lost, however, much of the energy that marks well-united and consolidated states, and must have had the constant mortification of seeing themselves without influence in the councils of Europe, which their real unity of nationality claimed, but their diversity of governments failed to secure. Whether the advantages are on the side of large or of small states ; whether the advantages of a divided Germany are to be counterbalanced by those of a united one, is a problem for future time.

History of Italy.—So far an attempt has been made

to indicate pretty continuously the national and feudal history as well as the imperial relations of Germany as they concerned the interior of German administration and the Slav neighbours. The history of Italy has been avoided, and the chief parallels and illustrations have been drawn from France and England—England as the allodial or national, France as the feudal model. Italian history cannot be learned without the previous understanding of German and French history. The relations of the empire and Papacy and of the Italian republics is not the history of Italy. North Italy was for many centuries Gallic before the Roman empire condescended to recognise it as Italian at all. And it ceased to be Roman or Italian and became Teutonic or Lombard, whilst many other provinces of Rome continued Roman. North Italy must be studied in the light of German history, and South Italy in the light of French history. It is curious that, except during the zenith of Roman imperialism (and till 1870), all Italy was never Italian in the sense of unity. North Italy was Lombard when South Italy was Greek. South Italy was Norman when North Italy was wavering between German and mongrel Italian. And southern Italy was as the Norman kingdom, a fine illustration of feudality, to be compared with England as a conquered feudalised country, the feudalism being here imposed on the miscellaneous aggregate of nationalities that all the tides of all conquests have swept into the favoured home of bandits and brigands, just as in England it was imposed on the intermixed but only intertribally mixed race of Low Germans after the modification of Danish conquest. In any discussion of German history in the succeeding centuries it will be necessary to investigate more carefully than has been done hitherto the constitutional part of that history; and it will be necessary to elucidate more clearly the relations with France as well as with Italy.

IMPORTANT DATES

Henry VI., 1190–1197.
Coronation at Rome, 1191.
Expedition to Southern Italy, 1191.
His coronation at Palermo, 1195.
Diet at Würzburg, 1196.
Sicilian rebellion suppressed, 1197.
Philip of Swabia elected Emperor (March), 1198.
Otto of Brunswick elected Emperor (May), 1198.
Death of Philip (June), 1208.
Otto is unanimously elected Emperor (November), 1208.
Frederick of Hohenstaufen (son of Henry VI.) accepts the German
      Crown, 1211.
Otto marries Beatrice of Hohenstaufen, 1212.
Battle of Bouvines (July 27), 1211.
Frederick II. undisputed Emperor, 1215–1250.

INDEX

Printed by BALLANTYNE, HANSON & Co.
Edinburgh & London